GOLD RUSH QUEEN

Camp along the Koyukuk River, Wiseman, Alaska, six miles (9.7 kilometres) from where Nellie Cashman lived for twenty years, c. 1915.

Gold Rush Queen

THE EXTRAORDINARY LIFE OF NELLIE CASHMAN

THORA KERR ILLING

TouchWood
Editions

Editing by Marlyn Horsdal
Cover and interior design by Pete Kohut
Cover images found in the public domain. Image of Nellie Cashman courtesy of
the Ben T. Traywick Collection; image of Tombstone, 1881, by C.S. Fly.

LIBRARY AND ARCHIVES CANADA CATALOGUING IN PUBLICATION
Illing, Thora Kerr, author
Gold rush queen : the extraordinary life of Nellie Cashman / Thora Kerr Illing.

Issued in print and electronic formats.
ISBN 978-1-77151-159-9

1. Cashman, Nellie, 1844–1925. 2. Women pioneers—West (US)—
Biography. 3. Pioneers—West (US)—Biography. 4. West (US)—Biography.
5. Frontier and pioneer life—West (US). 6. Frontier and pioneer life—
Arizona—Tombstone. 7. Tombstone (Ariz.)—Biography. I. Title.

F595.C342I45 2016   978'.02092   C2016-903305-8

We acknowledge the financial support of the Government of Canada through
the Canada Book Fund and the Canada Council for the Arts, and of the
province of British Columbia through the Book Publishing Tax Credit.

PRINTED IN CANADA AT FRIESENS

20 19 18 17 16   1 2 3 4 5

For Dorothea Maria Johnson (1922–2015)
wise woman and friend

CONTENTS

Nellie Cashman's tombstone in Ross Bay Cemetery, Victoria, BC.
PHOTO BY PETE KOHUT.

INTRODUCTION

REQUIESCAT IN PACE reads the grey granite plaque over the grave of Nellie Cashman, mining pioneer and philanthropist, in the Ross Bay Cemetery in Victoria, British Columbia. Anyone familiar with the picaresque life of the deceased may question whether Nellie would have wanted to spend eternity in peace. Certainly she was a good Roman Catholic, but she was incurably restless, working the mining camps of the United States and Canada for more than thirty years before settling in Alaska for the last twenty years of the long adventure that was her life.

The lure was silver and gold, and Nellie, like all long-time prospectors, believed that the big bonanza, the great strike, was always just over the next hill. There was always another prospect to investigate, another shaft to sink. It was exciting and it was addictive. Running a boarding house or a grocery provided the money to fund prospecting and mining, but for a woman of Nellie's mettle, that was not enough. She loved the talk of the camps, the respect she won, the thrill of the chase. Despite the hardships, she described mining as a romantic business and for her it was. She shared many traits with the best of the prospector-miners. They were tolerant and honest, they trusted each other, and they shared what they had.

Even before she found her métier in mining, Nellie knew she was not destined to be a servant or a factory girl, the fate of many young Irish famine emigrants. Determination shows in her portrait as a young woman, and that quality comes through again and again in her life story. Over the years she had some health setbacks, but she was physically as well as mentally tough. She lived to be eighty and was active until shortly before she died. She thought nothing of sleeping out in the snow, and for years she allowed herself only two blankets as coverings. At a time when well-bred women wore tight corsets and entertained one another at tea, Nellie was probably never happier than when camping out on a frozen river under the stars. She was in her mid-seventies when she made an extraordinary winter journey, mushing 750 miles (1,207 kilometres) in Alaska in seventeen days. After surviving a rafting accident on a swift river, her comment was, "There is always something interesting happening. You never quite know what's going to happen or when your time will come to cash in your checks. It all adds interest and variety to life." [1] In her obituary notice several newspapers, including the *Anchorage Weekly Times* and the *Fairbanks Daily Times*, quoted Nellie as saying, "I have mushed with men, slept out in the open, siwashed [camped out without a tent] with them and been with them constantly, and I have never once been offered an insult. You won't find that class of men among the sourdoughs of Alaska. A woman is as safe among them as at her own fireside. If a woman complains about her treatment from any of 'the boys,' you can take my word for it she has only herself to blame." [2] On another occasion she told Fred Lockley, a Portland journalist who became a friend, "I never have had a word said to me out of the way. The 'boys' would sure see to it that anyone who ever offered to insult me could never be able to repeat the offence."[3] She told Lockley that she had never carried a gun and would not know how to shoot one.

The *Klondike Nugget* paid tribute to Nellie's career in April 1900, saying, "There is not a mining camp in the country where she is not known and loved, as her many deeds of charity have endeared her to the hearts of all who ever knew her . . . Nellie . . . knows more about mining in all branches than many a man who poses as an expert."[4] Nellie was a self-educated geologist but learned her lessons well. Men came to respect her judgment, and superstitious miners saw her arrival in a camp as a sign of good luck.

The landscape of the narrative changed frequently, but there were constants too. Nellie's Roman Catholic faith was central to her life. Even in Alaska, far from a church and a religious community, she was spiritually at peace. She commented, "It takes the solitude of frozen nights with the howl of dogs for company; the glistening fairness of days when nature reaches out and loves you, she's so beautiful, to bring out the soul of folks."[5]

Nellie has a special place in the history of the Old West as a virtuous woman. She was endlessly generous. She made money but gave much of it away, to the Roman Catholic Church to build a hospital and to fellow miners who were down on their luck.

No hungry man was turned away from the several restaurants she ran, and she would dip into her own savings to help other mining hopefuls equip themselves for an expedition. Among the prospectors and miners of North America there were other kind women who cooked for and nursed men, but almost none whose ambition to make a fortune had no personal motivation. Nellie wanted money to make life easier for others.

When Nellie moved north of the Arctic Circle around 1904, she was one of a very small number of women to settle there. That did not worry her. She said to Lockley, "The further you go from civilization, the bigger-hearted and more courteous you find the men. Every man I met up north was my protector, and any man I ever met, if he needed my help got it, whether it was a hot meal, nursing, mothering, or whatever else he needed. After all, we pass this way only once, and it's up to us to help our fellows when they need our help."[6]

She was clearly good company, and she liked to laugh. A fellow prospector, Edward Morgan, who knew her well, commented, "She had the gift of palaver and was a most convincing talker."[7] Despite the camaraderie she enjoyed with kindred spirits and the compassion for the needy that infused her life, Nellie chose to journey alone. She made friends for life, but she did not need a husband for security or happiness.

Unfortunately, she left no written memoirs, although she did write letters to her sister and her favourite nephew, and she liked to give newspaper interviews. As she aged, her recollection of early events became slightly confused and perhaps embellished for the benefit of the press, but the essential fact is that this world was graced by an irrepressible and courageous woman, successful in a man's world and ahead of her time in her independence and self-reliance.

Few stampeders had the grit to mine and settle in the Arctic wilderness, but Nellie's peregrinations from south to north were typical of the search. The history of gold in the Americas runs from south to north, starting in pre-Hispanic times. In North America, the significant early gold strikes were in the mountains of the west. Prospectors followed hunches that the most promising deposits would be found farther north and, over the years, north they trekked, pushing on from the southwest to California and later on to the basin of the Yukon River in Canada and Alaska.

Fred J. Dodge, who worked as an undercover agent for Wells Fargo in Tombstone, stated, "Nellie Cashman was one of the most wonderful women I ever met. She was unique. Though she seemed to prefer to associate with men, there never was a spot on her moral character. I knew her in Nevada and in California before either of us reached Tombstone. In every place where I knew her she was the queen of the Irish miners and held the respect of the 'cousin Jacks' [Cornish miners] as well. Indeed this high opinion of her was held by all right thinking men . . . I have always regarded Nellie as a most remarkable and admirable woman."[8]

A rare photo of Nellie Cashman as a young
woman, as taken in San Francisco in 1874.

CHAPTER ONE
EARLY YEARS

N O BIRTH CERTIFICATE has been found for Nellie, but she was christened in October 1845, the first year of the Great Famine that was to kill eight hundred thousand people and cause the emigration of more than two million adults and children between 1845 and 1855, reducing the population of Ireland by a third. Nellie, or Ellen as she was christened, was the elder of two daughters of Frances and Patrick Cashman, who were probably tenant farmers.

Home for the Cashmans was either near Middleton (now spelled Midleton), 13 miles (22 kilometres) east of Cobh (Queenstown) in County Cork, or Belvelly, a small village about 4 miles (2.5 kilometres) north of Cobh. Midleton now claims Nellie as a native daughter. The small town lies in a fertile valley of the Owenacurra River. Before the potato famine it was good farming country. Cobh was known as Queenstown for over seventy years after a visit by Queen Victoria in 1849, a visit that was carefully orchestrated to show the queen's solidarity with her suffering subjects. For a state visit in the aftermath of the famine, it was largely a success. Prince Albert said of Cork that "delighted affection was everywhere seen."[1]

Nellie was probably born in August of 1845. Her gravestone gives the year 1844, but it is unlikely that her parents would have waited more than a year to christen her. Their firstborn, a son, died soon after his christening. After Nellie came a girl, named Frances after her mother. Frances, better known as Fanny, was probably still a baby when Patrick Cashman died, a death that may well be attributed to starvation or related disease, since County Cork was particularly hard hit by the famine. Like other tenant farmers of rural Ireland, the Cashmans almost certainly lived on a scrap of land, growing wheat, oats, and barley for sale and potatoes for their own use. When the potato harvest of 1845 was stricken by a killer fungus (*Phytophthora infestans*), it spread rapidly. Black spots appeared on the plant leaves, and a whitish mould showed on the underside. Wind and rain transferred the spores of the mould very quickly, and potatoes that looked sound would produce small spots in a matter of hours. The smell of diseased potatoes when boiled was evidently disgusting. By winter's end three-quarters of Ireland's potato crop was destroyed. It was the staple in the diet of the poor, and the Cork area ran short of food. In mid-April 1846, Ireland's leading newspaper, the *Freeman's Journal*, reported attacks on flour mills in Clonmel, County Tipperary, by "people whose bones protruded through the skin which covered them, staring through hollow eyes as if they had just risen from their shrouds." [2]

The *Cork Examiner* was equally graphic. In the winter of 1846 it reported, "Disease and death in every quarter—the once hardy population worn away to emaciated skeletons—fever, dropsy, diarrhoea and famine rioting in every filthy hovel and sweeping away whole families . . . every field becoming a grave and the land a wilderness." [3]

Faced with the calamity unfolding across the sea, Westminster gave some help. Men were employed on road gangs, but they were often too weak to work, especially in winter, and soup kitchens with official sanction were set up for a limited time only. It was too little relief, given too late. Within twelve months of the first appearance of the blight, a million and a half Irish men, women, and children were without food, searching the stubble fields for old stalks of potato. Ireland suffered three successive bad harvests, with 1848 being the worst; the new potato crop was almost totally lost to disease. Dysentery and fever often followed starvation, and funerals were constant, sometimes in mass graves, and there was no money for coffin or shroud.

For surviving tenant farmers, paying the rent was paramount, even at the cost of buying food. Default meant eviction, and landlords could be pitiless. People who could left the country, walking like skeletons to the ports. In 1847 alone a quarter of a million Irish left home. The Great Hunger cast a long shadow. Emigrants were frequently so damaged in health that they did not last long in the New World. Those who survived took with them bitter memories and an anger that would later find expression in the Fenian and other revolutionary movements fighting to create an independent Ireland, free of the hated landlords. As an adult, Nellie would not fly the Union Jack and claimed the American flag as her own. She named one of her earliest mining claims after the Irish patriot Charles Stewart Parnell.

In later life Nellie did not explain the exact circumstances of their emigration, but it seems likely that loss of the family farm after Patrick Cashman's death pushed his widow to flee to America. It was a bold move, but in that desperate time it was not unknown for widows and young children to board the ships leaving the stricken country. The first steamship had crossed the Atlantic from Cobh in 1848, and it was a well-used service, though dirty and crowded. Fares in steerage were relatively cheap, which was fortunate since most emigrants had little or nothing to take with them.

Nellie was about seven and Fanny three or four in 1852. Travelling to the small grey town of Cobh, now renamed Queenstown, and boarding a ship may have been exciting for them, but for Mrs. Cashman it was farewell forever to home and country, and she left behind the graves of her husband and their baby son.

———

LIKE MANY OTHER Irish emigrants, the Cashmans settled in Boston. In some ways it was not a good choice: New York might have been less of a challenge because of its ethnic diversity even in the mid-nineteenth century. Boston was an Anglo-Saxon city of some hundred and fifty thousand people, largely the descendants of English Puritans. In 1847, the first big year of emigration, thirty-seven thousand Irish Catholics arrived in Boston, almost all of them poor, unskilled except in farm or domestic work, and often ill from malnutrition. Squalid conditions on crowded ships helped to spread typhus and other fevers. Sick passengers were quarantined on an island in Boston harbour, and eight hundred died there, within tantalizing sight of the New World and its promise.

Weary passengers landing in summer faced heat and humidity of a kind quite unknown to them in rain-washed Ireland. Most came from a rural background, and now they were transplanted into hot, dirty city streets swarming with newcomers. The yearly inflow of immigrants was a huge challenge to Boston's settled community. They were not welcomed by the city's Protestants, some of whom could trace their ancestry to the *Mayflower*. Culture clash was inevitable.

Irish ghettos sprang up as immigrants crowded into tenements and cellars where they had the protection and comfort of shared experience. Men took whatever work they could find, all of it heavy.

The Irish cleaned out stables, worked as dock labourers, and dug canals. Wages were ten times what they could have earned in Ireland, but the work was gruelling and often dangerous. Moreover, the Irish had to compete for jobs with unskilled Boston men, sometimes freed slaves, who resented the willingness of the newcomers to work for less than the going rate. Irish women found work as servants and cooks to the affluent of Boston. It was an alien world to them. They knew nothing of the finer points of housewifery such as ironing and polishing silver, and their only experience was in cooking the most basic of foods. The girls either learned quickly or lost their jobs.

People of means found Boston a fine place to live. Rich merchants built themselves mansions to reflect their status, and the city was noted for its cultural life. But in the immigrant ghettos living conditions were appalling. Unscrupulous landlords divided big houses, such as the former homes of merchants, into warrens of tiny, airless rooms. Many of the Irish arrived sick; unsanitary housing compounded their misery, and diseases spread. The average adult Irish immigrant lived only six years after arriving in the United States, and six out of ten children born in the slums died before the age of six. Small wonder that some immigrants succumbed to alcohol and despair. Neglected children roamed the streets and crime soared.

Wealthy Bostonians reacted with horror and hostility. Animosity was widespread, fuelled by the suspicion that a Catholic's first allegiance was to the Pope. Anti-Catholic sentiment waned to some extent during the Civil War that tore apart the country between 1861 and 1865. The overwhelming majority of Irish immigrants supported the Union cause, and an Irish Brigade fought with distinction in major battles.

Despite the prejudice and hardship, the Irish who survived the early years in America saw it as a land that could offer opportunities impossible at home. They tended not to assimilate, at least in those early years. Clustered around their schools and churches, the immigrants married friends and neighbours and provided a natural support system for one another.

Mrs. Cashman and the girls spent more than ten years in Boston, living for at least part of the time on Federal Street in the south of the city not far from the harbour. She probably worked as a cook; she and Nellie were later to earn a living cooking for others. Somehow the girls acquired an education. Nellie in later life was known as an avid reader, and she certainly understood the power of advertising in print.

Nellie grew up spirited but naturally religious. Early on she showed a zest for work that never flagged. Because so many young men died on the battlefields or from related disease, the Civil War created opportunities for young women that would not have been open to them twenty years earlier. Nellie was able to get a job as an elevator operator in a public building. She was about sixteen at the time, pretty and spunky. She loved to talk, speaking with the Irish accent she never lost. After Nellie's death, a friend, John Clum, spoke warmly of her "emphatic and fascinating Celtic brogue."[4]

A story that became part of the Cashman legend has Nellie being advised to move out west by General Ulysses Grant of the Union army. Nellie supposedly told Frank Cullen Brophy, a banker and rancher in Arizona, "I remember when I met General Ulysses S. Grant. I was a bellhop in Boston at the time. He was easy to talk to, like anyone I ever knew, and when I told him I wanted to do things, because I had to if I wanted to live, he said, 'Why don't you go west, young woman? The West needs people like you.' Well, we had gone west when we left Ireland, and I certainly didn't expect to spend the rest of my life being a bellhop or an Irish servant girl here in Boston."[5]

Perhaps the general's words were all the encouragement the Cashman women needed. Nellie knew she was meant for more than domestic service or work in one of the mills of the eastern states. In factories, much of the pay the girls earned was swallowed by boarding, lodging, and laundry. House servants at least had a roof over their heads and meals, but the hours were long, and their comings and goings were strictly regulated. For a lass of independent spirit Boston held no appeal. Whether it was the general's advice or her own hard-headed assessment of her likely future in Boston, Nellie believed the west held better opportunities.

It was a plucky move for Mrs. Cashman and her daughters, since in the 1860s California was virtually a separate country. A prize of the war that ended the Mexican-American conflict, California had flown the American flag since 1848, but it was a territory without the infrastructure and laws that governed the east. Lawless or not, a city was growing along the shores of San Francisco Bay, and the town had an Irish community, though much smaller than Boston's.

The Cashmans left for the west coast in 1865 or 1866. In 1866 the *Boston City Directory* shows Mrs. Cashman still living at 328 Federal Street, but data must have been collected in advance of printing.

Had the Cashmans waited another three years they could have crossed the continent by train. The Union Pacific completed its hugely ambitious engineering feat in 1869, and passenger service began in May of that year.

Before then, for miners and others anxious to reach the west without braving Cape Horn or the long land journey through hostile Indian territory, there was another route. Far-sighted financiers in the eastern states had contracted with the government of New Granada (present-day Panama and Colombia) for the exclusive right to build a railroad across the Isthmus of Panama. Linked with steamship services on the Atlantic and Pacific coasts, a train would allow a quicker and safer route for mail, for the collection of silver and gold bullion on the Mexican coast, and for passengers. Starting in 1850, a forty-seven mile (seventy-five kilometre), single-track line was pushed across the isthmus. The cost in worker life was high, but in January 1855, the first train crossed the isthmus. Until the opening of the transcontinental railroad, the Panama route was a vital communication link between the two coasts for twenty years.

The four-hour ride through the jungle must have been astonishing to women who had known only rural Ireland and the streets of Boston. On the Pacific coast passengers transferred the same evening to a steamship bound for San Francisco. Sea voyages in the nineteenth century were rarely pleasurable, at least for steerage passengers. In the 1860s conditions on ships owned by the Cornelius Vanderbilt conglomerate came in for scathing criticism for over-crowding, and bad food and service. The British consul at Panama fumed, "It is beyond me to describe the nasty food, filthy table cloths, and dirty knives and forks."[6] Steerage passengers sometimes found that the places they were supposed to be allocated on deck had been pre-empted by sheep and cattle. Fortunately, the whole journey from New York or New Orleans to San Francisco could now be completed in about three weeks.

Even though the California gold rush of 1849 was long over, among the Cashman women's fellow passengers were young men who believed they could still make a fortune from a lucky strike. It was Nellie's first encounter with gold fever, and she clearly was not put off by rough manners, despite the fact that some of the travellers were wild young fellows carrying guns.

———

SAN FRANCISCO WAS first settled by the Spanish in the eighteenth century. Now flying the American flag, the old Spanish military post and religious mission was transformed by the gold rush of 1849 into a rough town of thirty-five thousand. The sandy bay became a place of tents, wooden buildings, and mining hopefuls, spurred on by ambition and dreams of striking it rich. A few married women accompanied their husbands to the goldfields, but in San Francisco women were few and working women a rarity.

By 1852 there were approximately forty-two hundred Irish in San Francisco, and by 1880 more than thirty thousand—one-third of the population. San Francisco had become the tenth-largest city in America. This critical mass gave the Irish influence in commerce and political life. It was easier than it had been back east to open a store or buy land. The year after the Cashmans arrived, San Francisco elected an Irish mayor, Frank McCoppin. The Irish were the only immigrant group to have their own bank, the Hibernia Savings and Loan Society, founded by James Phelan, an Irish-born entrepreneur who made money as a trader during the gold rush.

San Francisco was freer of anti-Catholic sentiment than the cities of the east. The Catholic Church and Irish newspapers helped forge a sense of identity, and Irish associations proliferated. They were cultural, religious, or economic, and they took care of widows and helped the sick. Even after the gold ran out in the 1860s, San Francisco was a promising place for young people with ambition.

The Cashman women settled in a boarding house on Fifth Street. This was a fateful move for Fanny, who fell in love there. Thomas J. Cunningham may have owned the boarding house, since he was already the president of a small but profitable boot-and-shoe manufacturing company, or he may have been simply a fellow boarder. Fanny was making a good match, because nothing was more essential to a prospector or miner than sturdy, well-fitting boots. Tom was born in County Cork, probably two or three years before Fanny, and like the Cashmans, he had spent some time in Boston. Tom did well in a modest way. Before he was thirty, he was secretary of the United Workingmen's Cooperative Boot & Shoe Company, and he went on to be its president, at least for a term. For Nellie, Tom's knowledge of the boot-and-shoe trade was to prove useful in her later business life, and she worked for a while in his factory.

Tom and Fanny married in 1870. Some acquaintances were surprised that vivacious, pretty Nellie had not married first, but she had her own ideas. Asked by a bold newspaper reporter in later years if she had never been tempted to settle down, Nellie replied that she had never cared for the notion of cooking for one man. She clearly saw marriage as a state that would crimp her longing for a free and self-reliant life. Nellie was correct in her judgment that marriage would keep her from adventures. For one thing, marriage brought babies: Frances had five of them within the decade.

Pioche, Nevada, 1881.

CHAPTER TWO

THE SOUTHWEST

TWO YEARS AFTER her sister married, Nellie and her elderly mother set out on the first step of what would be, at least for Nellie, a series of travel and work adventures. The gold rush in California was over, but in southeast Nevada silver mines were booming. The famous Comstock Lode of Virginia City made a fortune for some early prospectors, but there were other mining centres, commonly referred to as cities even when they were isolated desert camps. Nellie worked briefly as a camp cook in Virginia City, still rough-edged but somewhat settled after ten years in existence. Miners with money apparently appreciated her cooking. After a few months she and her mother headed for the Pioche district in the desert country of eastern Nevada. Here they bought out the owner of the Miner's Boarding House, at Panaca Flat, a milling camp about ten miles (sixteen kilometres) from Pioche.

Pioche was not a place for lone prospectors. Silver mining needed machinery. After the ore was mined, it was crushed and processed to reveal the precious silver, and that meant large-scale operations and mills. Like other boom-and-bust mining camps, Pioche's heyday lasted less than ten years, but for two or three years, its production of gold and silver, chiefly silver, was substantial. Pioche, including the outlying mill town of Panaca Flat, was a rowdy place. The *Pioche Daily Record* in October 1872 complained of refuse fouling the main street "packing cases, old boots, rags, discarded clothing, old wrapping paper and litter of every description meets the eye on every side." [1]

Pioche was not only filthy, it was violent. This was the Old West, where the gun was the law. Within a three-year period at least forty men died violently, mostly by gunshot. It was said that seventy-two graves were dug in Pioche before anyone died a natural death. Gunmen were drawn to Pioche, readily finding work as guards for the two rival mining companies or for men who had struck "pay dirt," the prospectors' term for an area where they had located precious metal. Robbery, stabbings, and shoot-outs with pistols were common among the young males, many of whom came from Ireland. One street fracas involved a young Jim Levy, born near Dublin, who went on to become one of the most feared gunfighters in the west. His opponent, David Neagle, the son of an Irish immigrant, later became a deputy US marshal.

When not working, the miners had a choice of seventy-two saloons and thirty-two brothels, but despite the dirt and violence, Pioche had churches, a school, and a hospital. The town also boasted a livery stable with three hundred horses, and a mule line connecting the camp with the coast. Nellie's spiritual home was the Roman Catholic Church, and the local newspaper in the fall of 1873 lists her as taking part in a bake sale and running a stall for cigars and refreshments to help Father Scanlan, her parish priest, raise funds for the church. For decades Nellie supported churches and hospitals with her own funds or by using her persuasive charm to get others to support causes dear to her heart.

By the spring of 1873 Nellie's name had replaced her mother's on advertisements for the boarding house. Mrs. Cashman was in her mid-seventies now, and she may have been pleased to relinquish active management to her daughter. The boarding house obviously made money, for they undertook some improvements. The *Pioche Daily Record* ran advertisements soliciting new business. "The proprietress of this house, having recently added to and materially improved the building for the accommodation of Boarders, respectfully returns thanks for past liberal patronage, and solicits an increase of Boarders, as she is prepared to accommodate all who desire *Good Board at Low Rates*. The Table will be supplied with the best to be had in the Market. N. Cashman."[2] Nellie was never one to hide her light under a bushel when promoting her kitchen.

Her guests were almost certainly fellow Irish. The other large ethnic group in mining communities of the west were Cornishmen, known as "Cousin Jacks," because when a mine needed more workers, they used to write home for a cousin to join them. From about 1840 on, the tin and copper mining industry in Cornwall had slumped, and hundreds of Cornish miners emigrated. They had no difficulty finding work in the coal and metal mines of America, for they were innovative and reckoned to be among the best hard-rock miners in the world. They knew how to sink shafts and trace gold-bearing veins through the rock, and one of the Cornish innovations was a pump to siphon water from underground recesses. They were proud, independent men, who sang lustily as they went to and from their shifts. Away from the mines their wrestling matches were legendary. To the Cousin Jacks, mining was an honourable profession, something one did for a working lifetime. The Irish, usually from a rural background and without mining skills, were recruited as labourers. For most, working in the mines was, they hoped, a stepping stone to better things. They would not stay with the dangerous, back-breaking work any longer than they had to.

Men working together in the same mine had to rely on each other, but above ground the Cornish and the Irish wanted the company of their compatriots, not to mention the kind of food they were used to. This meant that hotels and boarding houses attracted one group or the other but rarely a mix. They were great places for news and gossip. Here Nellie had the chance to acquire an understanding of what it took to be a prospector or a miner. She must have listened with interest to the talk around the dinner table, and she had the chance to ask questions.

In boarding houses of that time it was customary for the owner, often a widow, since mine accidents were frequent, to preside at the head of the main dining table, where seats were reserved for favoured guests. Younger or less important men sat at a second table. The miners slept in rooms off the entrance hall or upstairs. On hot and humid nights they were allowed to drag their mattresses out onto the wooden verandah, which extended around two or three sides of the building. Some boarding houses offered a bunk-house at the back for young men with less money.

From her boarders Nellie learned that it didn't take a lot of money to start out prospecting, but experience and luck both helped. Prospecting was the first stage of the hunt for gold, silver, or other valuable metals. A prospector's essentials were a pick, shovel, and pan, and these were readily available at any supply store. Assay houses sold other items such as mortars, pestles, and the horn spoon needed to wash panned concentrates. Some prospectors made their own pans with the help of blacksmiths. Most prospectors carried a rifle for protection or for hunting game, and on long trips a burro was useful to carry the outfit. Prospectors usually walked alongside, since if they were mounted, it was too easy to overlook promising mineralization. They were looking for "colour," the tint of earth or rock that indicated ore.

Placer or alluvial gold results from the weathering and wearing down of rock over eons of geological time. Moved on by water, it is often found in the gravel of stream beds, but also in terraces known as bench deposits on higher ground. For small-scale placer mining, no heavy machinery is needed; pioneer placer prospectors could get started on their own. At the most primitive level they pricked gold out of cracks in the rocks with a knife. If they had simple equipment, they filled a pan with gravel, swirled water into the pan, and rotated it by hand to float out the soil and sand as the heavier gold sank to the bottom of the pan. They would stand hour after hour in streams with their gold pans, swirling and washing to separate gravel from gold. A prospector might wash through fifty or more pans in a day; it took a strong back as well as patience.

A promising placer justified working a rocker or sluice at the site. Rockers speeded up the washing process, but it was easier with two or three men. The rocker was a wooden box, set on a slant, with ribs or partitions called riffle bars on the bottom in the lower half of the device. At the upper end, a hopper had sieve holes. As water was run through the rocker, rocks were kept out of the sieve and gold was trapped by the riffles. The sluice box, invented by Nevada miners, became the standard tool of the California gold rush, and its use spread north. A sluice was a series of wood or metal boxes, end overlapping end to form a long trough. Like the rocker, it had riffles to trap gold. Placed on an incline, the sluice might be anywhere from 100 feet (30 metres) to 1,000 feet (305 metres) in length. The idea was to channel the stream water that rushed downhill when summer melted the mountain snows. Prospectors still had to shovel pay dirt into the sluice boxes, but the rush of water dissolved clay and swept big stones and debris to the end of the run, where they formed the tailings pile. To help trap the gold, quicksilver was used at "clean up." The mix from the riffles was put into a buckskin bag, and the quicksilver was squeezed out or heated to get the last of the gold. Prospectors usually ran their sluice for a week before moving to "clean up." With good water flow, the process worked well, but in many mining camps there were no rushing streams. Then water had to be brought from the nearest source by flume or aqueduct, adding to the expense.

Later developments included mechanical scrapers in streams and the hydraulic mining of hillsides. Instead of digging and shovelling soil and ore by hand into a sluice, miners used a nozzle and hose to wash pay dirt from the hillside straight into the sluice. It cut out some hard work and was cost effective, but hydraulic mining was not suited to every site. In big operations whole hillsides were washed away, filling valleys with stones and mud, but the environmental costs were not recognized until later.

The more sophisticated mining became, the more it cost, but a lucky prospector could still do well. If he found a lode—a vein of metal ore in the earth's crust—away from the gravel streams, he could sell or lease his rights to a mining company that had the machinery needed to exploit the deposit.

It was all fascinating to Nellie, and she must have asked many questions. She learned that staking a claim was regulated by the government. The prospector had to hammer stakes into a parcel of land, typically 500 feet (150 metres) square, posting on one stake his name, the date, and the number of the claim. The first claim on a creek was known as Discovery, and subsequent claims were staked as No. 1 Above or No. 2 Below and so forth. The prospector then had to get to the nearest mining recorder's office to register his claim and pay the fee that made it official.

Nellie and her mother had arrived in Pioche in 1872, the peak year for silver and gold production. Five and a half million tons of metal left the camp that year. By 1876 production had dropped by 45 per cent. The Nevada mines felt the impact of a slump in the price of silver linked to inflation, bank failures, and investments gone sour in Europe and the eastern states. The resulting depression lasted from 1873 to 1879.

In response, Congress in 1873 changed its silver policy. Previously, the United States had backed its currency with both gold and silver and minted coins of both types. The Coinage Act of 1873 moved the country to a de facto gold standard. Thereafter, silver dollars would still be minted for export, but the Treasury no longer bought silver at a statutory price, nor bought silver from the public for conversion to coins. The new legislation immediately affected the silver mines of the western states. The demonetization of silver emptied camps and ruined miners who were previously doing well. James A. McKenna, a pioneer of the southwest, explained in his memoir *Black Range Tales*, "Most of the mines closed down, and men with means left the country. Those who had to stay for want of money, or because it was tied up in the mines, barely managed to get enough for bed and board. A few who had water on their claims took up either cattle or goats on shares, but many of the older men who were Civil War veterans went into a soldier's home or became a charge on the country or state." [3]

While profits were running out in Pioche, so were takings at the camp's boarding houses. When news reached town of a strike in the Panamint Mountains of California, miners left in droves, and Nellie and her mother decided it was time to go too. They were lucky to sell their boarding house to a firm called Jacobs & Sultan. It was a hard time for merchants and entrepreneurs, and the local court was kept busy selling goods on behalf of the insolvent. By November 1873 Nellie and her mother had left Pioche. They had been in the Panaca Flat camp for only sixteen months but Nellie was already showing a sure sense for buying and selling at the right time. She had run a successful business and supported her parish church, and it is likely she and her mother had money to bank when they returned to San Francisco. Just as important, Nellie had shown that even a good Catholic girl could handle the rough-and-tumble of life in a mining camp. In later camps, Nellie was known for a time as Nellie Pioche; she was already making a name for herself.

In later years she told her friend Frank Brophy, "Those miners were a rough lot, but they were good men. I liked them and they liked me, and if the silver veins had not begun to pinch out, I might have been there 'til I died. But that's the way it is in mining— just when you don't expect it, you strike it rich, and then when you think you are about to become a silver queen or a copper queen, the vein peters out and you hear there's a big new strike in Alaska or some other Godforsaken place."[4] Nellie was already showing her pragmatic acceptance of the shifts in fortune that went with mining and her willingness to move on to a better prospect.

Although she held no mining claims in Pioche, Nellie had learned that money could be made quickly, and she liked that idea very much. A settled base was not important to her. For more than thirty years she would move on wherever the siren call of a new strike enticed her. Something in her personality responded to excitement and the lure of the unknown. She shared many traits with the typical stampeder: she was restless, was careless with money once she made it, and found the egalitarian life of the camps appealing.

Mother and daughter, comfortably funded, relaxed for a few months in San Francisco, and the city became Mrs. Cashman's permanent home. Nellie, now nearly thirty, made time to have her photograph taken. She went to Edouart & Cobb's studio on Kearny Street, which produced a well-known photograph, one of only two to show her in her youth. The version known today is actually a painting of the original, a copy of which was taken to Hong Kong by Sam Lee, a Chinese cook who had been employed by Nellie. He must have had great respect for his employer to carry her picture with him and eventually return with a painted copy. The face in the portrait is lovely, but it is striking for the intensity of the direct gaze. Eventually the portrait passed to her favourite nephew and hung on the wall of his home in Arizona.

Nellie enjoyed spending time with her mother and sister, but San Francisco could not hold her for long. Early in 1874 she joined a group of miners from Nevada to go prospecting. She later told Fred Lockley, an Oregon journalist, "In 1874 I went to San Francisco where I joined a party of six adventurous spirits who were outfitting to go to the mines. Some of them wanted to go to South Africa, some wanted to go to the newly discovered mines in British Columbia. We tossed up a coin, heads for South Africa, tails for British Columbia. It fell tails up so we went North." [5]

Panning for gold at Nome, Alaska, c.1900.
IMAGE E-01003 COURTESY OF ROYAL BC MUSEUM AND ARCHIVES.

CHAPTER THREE

THE CASSIAR

A ND SO THE first great adventure of Nellie's life
was decided by the toss of a coin. It is typical
of the prospector spirit that she and her
Pioche friends could treat their future in such a cav-
alier fashion. South Africa was forgotten in favour
of the mountain country drained by the turbulent
Stikine River in northwest British Columbia. Placer
gold was first mined in the Cassiar region by a
French Canadian, Alexander "Buck" Choquette.
His success was celebrated in the press in Victoria,
and a few hundred men tried prospecting along the
banks of the Stikine. It was wild country and, before

Choquette, very little known except to the Stikine Tlingit people.

Choquette's strike was actually a modest one and he fared better as a trader, but in 1873 another French Canadian, Henri Thibert, made a bigger strike, this time on the west side of Dease Lake. Thibert and a partner, McCullough, found gold in one of the creeks feeding into the lake. It was a notable discovery, enough to cause excitement up and down the coast when word leaked out. Even as far south as Nevada there was news of the Cassiar strike. Nellie probably attended meetings held by miners in Pioche to talk about it and make plans, and in San Francisco she made a point of reading the *Mining & Scientific Press*, the leading mining paper of the west.

Hundreds of miners headed to the Cassiar in 1873. In later years, Nellie said that she went to the Cassiar with two hundred miners from the Comstock camp in Nevada and that she was the only woman in the party. She probably meant that she and her six companions linked up with other prospectors sailing north from San Francisco. What is striking is that veteran miners accepted a young woman, but there seems to have been a consensus that she was sensible and self-reliant and up to the rigours of travel in rough country. Nellie was not much more than 5 feet (152 centimetres) in height and slightly built, but she never let her physique prevent her from taking on challenges. Fellow prospectors understood that her iron will more than compensated for what she lacked in height and weight.

She and the men provisioned themselves with much of the equipment and clothing they would need and sailed north to Victoria. There they bought blankets and food. Situated at the southern end of Vancouver Island, Victoria was barely twelve miles (nineteen kilometres) from the American mainland across the Strait of Juan de Fuca. The Fraser River gold rush had changed the trading post forever, and by the 1870s a few enterprising merchants were well equipped to handle mining expeditions.

Suitably provisioned, Nellie and her companions found places on one of the infrequent steamers bound for Fort Wrangell, 800 miles (1,288 kilometres) north in Alaska, a three-day voyage that took them through some of the world's most spectacular coastal scenery. Wrangell was a rowdy American trading post, well positioned near the mouth of the Stikine River, the waterway that cut through the coastal mountains and led into the interior of northwest Canada and southeast Alaska. For the Tlingit people, who had lived in the area for centuries, Stikine meant "great river." The Stikine valley was then, and long remained, one of the great untamed wilderness regions of the continent.

In Wrangell the group arranged passage on a small boat which took them 160 miles (318 kilometres) upriver to Buck's Bar, later renamed Telegraph Creek, the head of navigation on the river. Buck's Bar was a Hudson's Bay trading post and here, of course, they were in Canadian territory. Prospectors then had to load their goods onto sleds for a long cross-country hike of nearly 100 miles (161 kilometres). They travelled in early summer, but the trails were primitive and there were mountains to cross. Even for a man in robust health the journey was challenging.

On the west side of Dease Lake a small tent camp was emerging, known variously as Laketon and Dease Town. Here Nellie and her companions camped while building log cabins. Dease and Thibert creeks were quickly staked, but in 1874 gold was found on McDame Creek, triggering a rush there. McDame, a creek flowing southeast into the Dease River, was to go down in the history books as the site of the largest solid gold nugget ever recorded in British Columbia. It was dug out of the ore in 1877 and weighed seventy-two ounces (two kilograms).

Nellie's companions went off to prospect for gold while Nellie opened a boarding house and saloon. In that isolated place, with a good cook in the kitchen, it was bound to be successful, although once again Nellie had the challenge of providing meals far from an urban centre. There were about fifteen hundred prospectors in the area that summer. The small settlement was a busy place, where log cabins replaced at least some of the original tents. Nellie was not the only person catering to the miners. At the height of the boom Laketon had five stores, four hotels or boarding houses, two cafés, and its own newspaper.

The government contracted labourers to build a trail from Telegraph Creek to Dease Lake. The trail not only eased the journey for prospectors, but also allowed cattle and horses to be driven overland from the cattle farms of Ashcroft on the banks of the Thompson River in the south Cariboo. Some animals were brought by boat to Glenora, the first Hudson's Bay post on the river, just a few miles downstream from Telegraph Creek. The small settlement of Telegraph Creek took its name from a telegraph line, proposed but never built, that was to connect North America to Europe through Siberia.

At Dease Lake, for the first time, Nellie became a miner, prospecting along the creeks while still cooking for her guests. Talk in her boarding house gave Nellie access to information about promising claims, and she proved adept at buying them at propitious moments. She also began to "grubstake": backers who trusted the integrity of a prospector or judged that his claim held promise would put up money for supplies, knowing that they would get a percentage of the profits if and when he struck pay dirt. In some cases backers did get rich and in others returns were meagre.

Nellie had had no Cassiar gold strike, but as a learning experience in several aspects of mining, her time at Dease Lake was valuable. The boarding house did well. By late fall 1874 Nellie felt affluent enough to leave for the winter, intending to return to the Cassiar in the spring. Back at Fort Wrangell she boarded the ss *Californian* and sailed south. The steamer carried three hundred thousand dollars in gold dust from the Cassiar mines, and part of that belonged to the lone woman on board. At Nanaimo, heavy fog halted the vessel, and Nellie and others continued on to Victoria by canoe. By now she was sufficiently newsworthy to rate a mention in the press. A reporter interviewing her for the *Daily British Colonist* of Victoria in February the following year noted, "Miss Nellie Cashman was one of the few white women who reached Cassiar last year, where she opened a boarding house on Dease Creek and realized a comfortable 'pile.'"[1]

It might have been a comfortable winter for Nellie in Victoria, renewing her friendships among the Catholic religious, but in early December news reached Victoria that the miners still in the Cassiar, and there were many of them, were unable to leave. A particularly severe winter had prevented their departure and stopped supplies from reaching them through the mountains. They were trapped, and scurvy was said to be spreading. Without hesitation Nellie persuaded and hired six men to accompany her back north. It was a heroic gesture and it was madness. Nellie had never known a northern winter, and she could have had little idea except from hearsay of what lay ahead. In mid- or late December they sailed north for Fort Wrangell with 1,500 pounds (680 kilograms) of food, chiefly the potatoes and lime juice known to cure scurvy if taken in time.

Back along the Stikine trails they went on snowshoes, each pulling a laden sled. The snow was too soft and deep to use dogs. It was incredibly hard work, plodding on day after day through what Jack London memorably described as "the white silence."[2] Often the trail was lost under the snow. The forests were dense, and icy winds swept off snow-laden mountains. Some days they could travel only five miles (eight kilometres). The cold numbed the body and the mind, and breathing was painful. Even if her companions took heavier sled loads, Nellie must have been pulling about two hundred pounds (ninety kilograms) of provisions, along with the two blankets she allowed herself for the bitter nights.

They had little to fear from bears, which were hibernating, and apparently wolves kept their distance, but one night an avalanche struck the camp, carrying Nellie a quarter of a mile (0.4 kilometre) downhill and burying her deeply. Nellie, who believed she had a guardian angel at her shoulder, dug hard and emerged undeterred. The cold was particularly intense that year all along the coast and, hearing that a party of prospectors and a woman were trying to reach Dease Lake, in late January the commander of Fort Wrangell sent out a party of soldiers to find them.

The soldiers found Nellie and her companions camped on the frozen Stikine River. Nellie was cooking supper on a wood fire and humming cheerfully. She declined their offer of escort back to the coast. As the *Daily British Colonist* reported later, "So happy, contented and comfortable did she appear"[3] that the soldiers allowed her to continue her journey. Nellie told Fred Lockley that the Wrangell commander had expected the party to be dead and had sent soldiers to retrieve her body for Christian burial. Nellie appreciated the gesture and offered the soldiers tea, according to some newspaper reports, or a good feed, as she recalled for Lockley.

A brave man carrying mail from Dease Lake to Wrangell encountered the party in mid-February and reported later meeting "the famous Nellie Cashman. The woman was on snowshoes and was as jolly as a sandbuoy [sic]. At the Boundary Post [Buck's Bar] she lost the trail, and was twenty-eight hours exposed to the pitiless pelting of a storm, without shelter or blankets." [4]

The terrible journey inland from the coast took seventy-seven days, but Nellie and her men, arriving in late February or early March, were in time to save numbers of the miners. The *Daily British Colonist* of February 5, 1875, lauded Nellie's "extraordinary freak [sic] of attempting to reach the diggings in midwinter," [5] and the story passed into legend. It may have been an act of insanity, and Nellie's friends certainly thought so, but it was very brave. From then on mention of Nellie's name brought respect. As her gravestone shows, Nellie Pioche was thereafter known as "the Angel of the Cassiar."

There may have been as many as seventy-five men hungry and ill. Scurvy is caused by a deficiency of vitamin C and affected all the mining camps where fruit and vegetables were scarce or unobtainable. It was a horrible disease, the great killer of the north country, progressing from chronic muscle and joint fatigue to skin sores, then hemorrhaging, and finally loss of teeth and black, swollen limbs. Death was excruciating. A few of the "sourdoughs," the term for the seasoned prospectors of the north, knew that spruce needles, twigs, and bark made up in a tea would ward off scurvy, and the Aboriginal peoples certainly did, but the old remedy was not widely used. Some prospectors and traders married or lived with Aboriginal women who kept them healthy, but most carried the infection of the white man's superiority and derided Native lore.

Once the men were well, or at least better, Nellie reopened her Dease Creek boarding house. It prospered, and she was able to send her mother five hundred dollars in gold, a substantial gift at a time when a square meal cost about twenty-five cents. Nellie was becoming known for her generosity, and not only to her family. In the summer of 1875 she made a tour of outlying camps in the Cassiar, gathering donations for the hospital of St. Joseph's that was being built in Victoria by the Sisters of St. Ann, a teaching and nursing order from Quebec that was to become a significant religious presence in the northwest.

Victoria lay 800 miles (1,288 kilometres) to the south, but Nellie now had a reputation as a heroine and was becoming adept at charming money or gold from the pokes of miners for the causes she took on. When she left the Cassiar for good in May 1876, she took with her five hundred and forty-three dollars for her good friends, the sisters.

The Cassiar mines were rich, but the good ore was quite quickly worked out. The value of production from the mines, a million dollars in 1874, was less than half that just three years later. For an astute businesswoman, Dease Creek was no longer the place to be. Nobody was staking new claims, guests were fewer, and the more ambitious prospectors were moving on. Nellie sold, or perhaps leased, her boarding house, followed the trails she now knew well, and then took a small boat back along the Stikine to Wrangell. Under early summer skies it was a different world from the one she had traversed so painfully eighteen months earlier. This time, from the boat, she had a chance to admire the river and the mountains, still carrying the weight of winter snows.

By mid-June Nellie was in Victoria, with time to visit the nuns and learn about their hospital-building project. The following year, St. Joseph's opened its doors in the heart of the town, and by 1908, after three additions, it could serve 150 patients. The nuns never forgot Nellie's financial backing.

Returning to San Francisco, Nellie was reunited with her mother and her sister. Fanny's family was growing; she and Thomas became parents to five children in the eleven years of their marriage. But Nellie found it hard to settle. She had proved she was a woman of unusual courage, able to hold her own in the company of rugged men. There were women, of course, in the mining camps—a small number of wives and even a few businesswomen—but most were prostitutes. Nellie had made it clear that she was not interested in courtship, and men respected the boundaries she set on friendship. From time to time Nellie, a pretty woman when she was young, was asked why she had not married. It was a question that made her laugh, and she used to brush it off, telling interviewers that she had always been too busy to talk about such things. When Bernice Cosulich, a Tucson journalist, interviewed Nellie for the *Arizona Daily Star* a year before her death, Nellie told her, "Men are a nuisance anyhow, now aren't they? Men, why child, they're just boys grown up. I've nursed them, embalmed them, fed and scolded them, acted as mother confessor and fought my own with them and you have to treat them just like boys."[6]

The Cassiar rescue placed Nellie firmly in the legends of the north country. Those who knew her well understood that her religious faith was the wellspring of her compassion. Others saw in her a remarkable young woman, capable of exploits that few would undertake.

Fourth and Fremont streets in Tombstone, 1882.

CHAPTER FOUR

ARIZONA

AFTER A YEAR Nellie moved to Tucson, a small community in the Santa Clara valley of southern Arizona. She had a sure instinct for an opportunity, and Tucson had potential. The Southern Pacific Railroad had opened the line between Los Angeles and Yuma in 1877, and in March 1880 the service was extended to Tucson. Once that happened prospectors, entrepreneurs, and prostitutes poured in. Even though there were as yet no mines of note in the area, Tucson was likely to become a transportation and commercial centre. Businesses opened, and the population increased five-fold.

Nellie knew something of Nevada from her Pioche days, but this was southern Arizona Territory, close to the border with Mexico, and the population of Tucson was largely Hispanic. The area had been inhabited for centuries by Native Americans. Jesuit priests and soldiers arrived in the seventeenth century to win souls and land for God and the Spanish crown, and Tucson became one of two Spanish missions in the area. After Mexico's independence from Spain, Tucson became part of Mexico, and a road from the village ran all the way to Mexico City. Tucson was captured by the US army during the Mexican-American war and came under the American flag officially at the end of that conflict.

Nellie boarded the train in Los Angeles in 1879. Years later she told a reporter that her chief memory of that city was of dogs. "There was nothing, absolutely nothing but dogs in sight," she exclaimed. So much for Los Angeles! Curiously, for a Catholic of that time, she added, "It was the first time I knew that animals had souls."[1] She transferred to a stagecoach in Yuma, remembering later the mosquitoes there that swarmed her dinner. October was a good month to arrive in Tucson. It could be hot and dusty, but Nellie had missed the extreme heat of the summer months. Though rapidly changing, Tucson was still a sleepy Mexican backwater. Clara Spalding Brown, a miner's wife with a gift for writing, who lived for a time in Tucson, described it in 1880 as "an odd city, more like an ancient Bible town than anything else, with its narrow streets, and rows of low-walled, flat-roofed adobes."[2] The streets had no sidewalks and, as in Los Angeles, stray dogs ran wild. A problem for building was the lack of trees. As men swarmed in from California and the eastern states, many of the new buildings had to be constructed of packing cases from goods unloaded from the train. But a few new hotels and saloons opened, and with the saloons came professional gamblers.

Churches, both Roman Catholic and Protestant, were there too. The Catholic Church had a long history in Arizona Territory and the adjoining Mexican state of Sonora. Seven Sisters of St. Joseph of Carondelet, a French order, had come to Tucson in 1870 to open schools, but they were asked to serve in the town's small hospital, opened in 1880. The nuns accepted the mission, and the hospital took in sick and injured railroad workers, among other patients.

Tucson was undeveloped, but the promise was there, which favoured a woman of Nellie's entre-preneurial instincts. She made her assessment of the town, could see that a restaurant would do well,

over the lease of a building on the south
e church plaza. The location was central,
Augustine Church (later cathedral) and
rom a mine, making it convenient for the
w.... . In the summer of 1879 Nellie opened the
Delmonico Restaurant, presumably named for
the famous New York establishment. It was to be
Nellie's favourite name for a restaurant. Her advertisement promised "The Best Meals in the City"
and that Miss Cashman, an experienced restaurateur, would "personally superintend the cooking
and dining arrangements." [3]

Tucson had a newspaper, the *Tucson Daily Citizen*,
and Nellie made an impression on young John Philip
Clum, its proprietor. They were to become friends.
Aged thirty-four, self-confident and pretty, Nellie
appeared in his office bearing her advertisement.
Clum was surprised but impressed. Tucson had few
non-Hispanic women and no other wanting to open
her own business. He wrote in his 1931 tribute, *Nellie
Cashman: The Angel of the Camp*, "Her frank manner,
self-reliant spirit, and her emphatic and fascinating
Celtic brogue impressed me very much. I had the
feeling that she would not only undertake but achieve
along lines that would be regarded as difficult and
daring by a majority of the weaker sex." [4]

Nellie's concern for people in need was evident to everyone who knew her. Speaking of the Tucson days, Clum noted that "as the proprietress of a public eating house she met a majority of the passing throng and was able, in her own quiet but effective way, to assist many a wanderer who was in need of a word of sympathy and encouragement, or perchance, of more substantial aid when one was down on his luck. And if any were in actual want, or sick, then Nellie was in her element, working out ways and means to relieve the needy and care for the afflicted."[5]

Nellie and Clum shared an enthusiasm for life and the ability to change career and location when a better opportunity beckoned. Clum, an Easterner, had previously been an Indian agent and had built a reputation for integrity and fair dealings with the Apache. A military coup for which he was long remembered was the capture, without bloodshed, of the Apache leader Geronimo. Clum's success did not endear him to the US army professionals, however, and he had poor support from the Indian Bureau. After three years, disillusioned, he resigned his post and became a newspaperman. Later, he became a senior official in the US Postal Service.

THE DELMONICO WAS successful but did not hold Nellie's attention for long. A lone prospector, Ed Schieffelin, had found silver in the hills of southeast Arizona in 1877. As soon as he filed his claim in Tucson, word was out, and from all over the west, men moved in great numbers to the place he named Tombstone. Within two years, Tombstone had a population of five thousand, and Nellie could not resist the excitement. She sold her lease on the Delmonico to a widow and bought a stagecoach ticket to Tombstone, 75 miles (121 kilometres) to the east. She later told a nephew's family that the man who took the seat beside the driver that day was Wyatt Earp. They were to become friends.

Most mineral strikes in the Old West were the result of dogged perseverance. Ed Schieffelin deserved his success. He had been smitten by gold fever as a boy, and for years he roamed Nevada, California, and Idaho, working as a teamster or mine labourer to save enough to fund his next prospecting venture. In 1877, when he was nearly thirty years old, he took a job as a scout or lookout at an army post, Camp Huachuca, in Arizona Territory, on the fringe of dangerous Apache country. Despite discouraging comments from men of the camp that he was likely to find only his tombstone out on the treeless plateau,

Schieffelin prospected when he could. It was a brave act in that landscape with the threat of ambush.

His persistence paid off when he traced promising mineralization to a vein of silver. Down to his last thirty cents, Schieffelin packed up his ore samples and headed north to find his brother, Al, then working at the Signal silver mine in the northwest of the territory. Here the brothers met Richard Gird, a mining engineer who had just started work at the Signal. He assayed Ed's specimens and found them to be virtually pure silver-lead. Gird, who had some money, became the brothers' partner on the strength of a handshake. The trio rode south to comb the hills and desert around Tombstone, staking first the huge silver deposit they named the Lucky Cuss. A second find became the Toughnut mine, while a third, discovered by another prospector, became the Contention-Grand Central mine.

For a time Tombstone was the richest mining camp in America. Even though the good ore ran out as the mines hit the very high water table, the Tombstone mines produced about six million dollars a year during the decade of their heyday. The mines and associated mills were funded with capital from San Francisco and eastern cities. Here the miner without money became a labourer.

Just a year after a townsite was laid out, brick, frame, and adobe buildings were replacing tents. Lumber had to be brought in from mountains to the east that were in the stronghold of Apache warriors, and water was a problem for residents until pipes were laid out to the Huachuca Mountains, but the town's future looked bright. Wells Fargo brought in mail and took out bullion or bars of silver. Western Union opened a telegraph office, giving Tombstone another lifeline to the outside world. In 1880 the railroad reached Benson, twenty-five miles (forty kilometres) to the south. Now stagecoaches could freight supplies to Tombstone in less than six hours, about half the time it had taken from Tucson. Early in 1881 Tombstone became the county seat. The town now had a population of six thousand, and by the end of the year another four thousand optimists had arrived.

Saloons were numerous. In 1880 alone more than one hundred liquor licences were issued, and fourteen faro tables ran twenty-four hours a day, faro being the game of choice in the Old West. The dance hall girls and prostitutes always had customers. The miners were mainly young and single, and they had money to burn. They were tough and they had to be, but it was the ranch hands who had the reputation for wild sprees when they were able to escape into town. Unruly they might be, but until 1881 men obeyed the ban on carrying arms in the streets. Guns had to be checked in at the doors of Tombstone's saloons.

The boom years lasted from 1879 to 1885 and reunited many of the prospectors who had previously worked the mining camps to the west. Nellie came to know and like the Schieffelin brothers, and also Wyatt Earp and his brothers. Her admirer, John Clum, started a newspaper, the *Tombstone Epitaph*, which became the rival to the already established paper, the *Tombstone Nugget*. As time went on the two papers represented sharply different interests. The *Epitaph* came to side with the law and order movement while the *Nugget* supported the politicos of the area.

Nellie's first venture in Tombstone was a store on Allen Street. Opened in April 1880, it sold a variety of goods for men and women, including boots and shoes. She called her store The Nevada Boot & Shoe Store, to give it the legitimacy of implied past connections with the mining community, the prime market for boots. The *Tombstone Nugget* gave her new venture a warm welcome, noting that Nellie had owned "the famous Delmonico restaurant in Tucson." The report continued, "as Nellie was never outdone in any business she has undertaken, her success in our midst is double sure. Call at her place of business."[6] Footwear was certainly a change from the restaurant business, but Nellie was not averse to trying something new. She had worked in her brother-in-law's factory in San Francisco, and she probably bought boots and shoes from him wholesale. Besides footwear the store sold cigars and tobacco, hats for men, and much else as befitted a "general furnishing goods emporium where every article for Gents' Ladies' and Children in the above line, can always be found."[7]

A short partnership with another Irish girl, Kate O'Hara, ended on amicable terms, and with a Tucson friend, Jennie Swift, Nellie added a second business, the Tombstone Cash Store, which sold groceries and other provisions. She and Jennie worked out of the same building on Allen Street. The store had a prime location between Fifth and Sixth streets, and the partners claimed it received fresh fruit daily from Los Angeles. Nellie was soon able to buy out her friend. Meanwhile, back in San Francisco, Kate O'Hara acted as Nellie's buying agent. Tea, coffee, and spices were the main purchases from San Francisco, while Los Angeles provided most other groceries. Many of the customers were miners. Their wages were often in arrears, so Nellie followed the usual practice of grocery and dry goods stores, allowing purchase on credit.

Advertising for the boot store disappeared from the Tombstone newspapers by the summer of 1881, and the business may have closed, but by then Nellie had leased the Arcade Restaurant from Joe Pascholy. Pascholy was an extremely successful Swiss immigrant, who at various times owned a mine in the Huachuca Mountains and one-third of another. He also had a stake in the popular Occidental Saloon, and he owned a building lot and an adobe house in town. At heart he was a cattle man, and he had a spread out in the Dragoon Mountains. He and Nellie got along well and were involved in other business deals over the years. The Arcade was a good opportunity for Nellie. It was in the same block as the town bank, the Safford & Hudson Bank. Less advantageous perhaps was its proximity to the Oriental Saloon, where young fellows out on a spree rode their horses up to the bar. However, the Oriental was part-owned by Wyatt Earp, a man Nellie knew she could trust, and she became a friend of his main partner, Milt Joyce.

Nellie placed her first advertisement in the *Nugget*. It read, "Again at my old occupation. Having had years of experience in the restaurant business I know whereof I speak, that the Arcade will serve Better Meals than any House in Town."[8] Nellie was never one to sell herself short. The restaurant specialized in steaks and chops.

Soon after she leased the Arcade, Pascholy sold it at a profit to a businessman from Pennsylvania, but that made little difference to Nellie's daily life. Frequent change was woven into the fabric of mining camps. Partnerships formed and dissolved; hotels and restaurants often changed ownership; last year's restaurant chef might be next year's owner. Despite running a new enterprise, Nellie found time to involve herself in civic affairs. Tombstone had a school but no hospital or Roman Catholic church. For Nellie, no town should be without a Catholic church, and in Tombstone, the Irish were the majority ethnic group. The bishop, who lived in Tucson, promised a priest if she could raise the funds. Nellie knew that she was good at fundraising and foresaw no problem.

On September 25, 1880, the *Tombstone Epitaph* noted, "Nellie Cashman, the irrepressible, started out yesterday to raise funds for the building of a Catholic church. We don't know what success attended her first effort but will bet that there is a Catholic church in Tombstone before many days if Nellie has to build it herself."[9] Nellie did not need to pick up a saw or hammer, but she did the rounds seeking contributions. The church was not difficult to sell among the Irish, and she also found donors among the silver mill workers of nearby communities. In a week Nellie raised seven hundred dollars, but more was needed. Her answer was that Tombstone needed theatre. She organized a musical comedy, *The Irish Diamond*, and its takings covered most of the additional funds needed for the church. Fund trustees were appointed and meetings were held.

A lot was available on the northwest corner of Safford and Sixth streets, and a request went out to tender. An adobe building went up, with a church at street level and a rectory above. The first of the promised priests, Father Antonio Jouvenceau, took up his duties, and the Sacred Heart of Jesus Church was dedicated in January 1881. The following year a wooden church was built, so the earlier building could be used solely as a rectory. Again Nellie led the building campaign and, according to parish history, she herself borrowed horses and a wagon to bring timber in from the mountains fifty miles (eighty kilometres) away. The *Epitaph* noted, "Miss Nellie Cashman, to whose zealous, active work much of this success has been due, desires us to thank the public for the generous manner in which they responded to her calls for aid in this worthy cause." [10]

In the midst of all this Nellie found time to push for a hospital. She became the treasurer of the Miners' Hospital Association committee and helped draft its bylaws and constitution. A hospital for Cochise County opened its doors early in 1881 and offered temporary nursing care. That summer Nellie went to Tucson and returned with three Sisters of Mercy, an order long established in Arizona, and they took over the running of the hospital. Many early patients were tubercular and, since this was the Old West, others had gunshot wounds.

Even with so much happening, Nellie supported Irish causes. When the Schieffelin Hall was inaugurated on St. Patrick's Day in March 1881, the big event was an Irish National Land League ball, the first of two that year. Known to Gaelic speakers as Conradh na Talún, this political organization had been founded in Ireland two and a half years earlier to abolish the absentee landlord system in Ireland and enable tenant farmers to own the land they worked. Nellie was one of the ball's organizers. She was young when she emigrated, but she remembered Ireland as a place of want and oppression. The league was dear to her heart, and she was glad to be a committee member of the Tombstone chapter. Writing about the St. Patrick's Day ball, the *Epitaph* enthused, "The thanks of an oppressed and kindred people are due to Miss Nellie Cashman, whose every heartbeat throbs in sympathy with suffering humanity the world over. Long and prosperous may her days be is the prayer of her friends here, which means the entire population of Tombstone." [11]

In later years John Clum commented of Nellie, "If she asked for a contribution, we contributed. If she had tickets to sell, we bought tickets. If she needed actors for a play, we'd volunteer to act. And although Nellie's pleas were frequent, none ever refused her." [12] Nellie knew everyone, and when she went out collecting for charity no one escaped. There might have been an unwritten rule about which side of the street to walk on, but Nellie visited the bars and theatres as readily as the more respectable hotels and restaurants. She had only to walk into the Oriental Saloon, or the Bird Cage Theater, where prostitution flourished behind the scenes, for the patrons and girls to know they had better reach into their pockets.

Perhaps even Nellie found her energies scattered. In June she placed a notice in the *Nugget*, "Having leased the Arcade Restaurant to Mr. I.A. Korka, I hereby announce that I have retired from business. It is important that all outstanding accounts be settled immediately. Thanking my old friends for past favours, I hope they will bestow their patronage upon my successor." [13]

Three weeks later fire raged through Tombstone, as so frequently happened in a time of oil lamps and wooden buildings. It began in the Oriental Saloon where, the story goes, men smoking cigars were unwisely measuring the contents of a liquor barrel. After the explosion that followed, half the businesses of Tombstone were engulfed in flames. The Arcade was burned to the ground, along with another forty or more buildings. Tombstone residents were resilient, and in a month much had been rebuilt. The mines were producing well, and Tombstone was still a town with a future.

Nellie had been looking around for a new business and, excited by news that Bisbee, a small mining town forty miles (sixty-four kilometres) to the south, was now working a superb copper deposit, she leased the Bisbee Hotel. It was one of her few business mistakes. In time, Bisbee would prosper, but Nellie was too early. Like silver, copper needed capital for milling and processing, and Bisbee was off the beaten track, almost in Mexico. In a matter of months Nellie returned to Tombstone. She was behind on rent in Bisbee, and the case went to the Cochise County court for settlement.

Nellie had other concerns at this time. In February 1881 her brother-in-law, Tom Cunningham, died of tuberculosis in San Francisco. He was not yet forty, and he left Fanny with five children, ranging in age from one to eleven. Nellie believed that Tombstone was still a town of opportunity and, despite an escalating feud between lawmen and rustlers, she urged her sister and the children to join her there. By late summer Aunt Nell was helping them settle in. Fanny shared the family work ethic, and she probably had money from the boot-and-shoe business. Together, the sisters took out a lease on a boarding house on the north side of Fremont Street, between Fourth and Fifth streets. They made extensive renovations, had the interior painted, and bought furniture. Early in October the Delmonico Lodging House opened for business. The owner was listed as Mrs. T.J. Cunningham, sister of Miss Nellie Cashman. Advertisements claimed "the most pleasant rooms in the city in a boardinghouse" that "will be kept cleanly, in the best of style." [14]

About this time Russ House, a newish boarding house and restaurant on the corner of Toughnut and Fifth streets, came up for sale. It was too good an opportunity to miss. Nellie's old business partner Joe Pascholy bought Russ House, and Nellie joined him. It was a partnership that would last six years, although at times Nellie sold her interest, and Pascholy was chiefly involved as financier and the supplier of meats from his cattle ranch. Shortly after the boarding house opened, the *Epitaph* ran a feature article, assuring readers that "the homelike features of the Russ House will be appreciated in a land where homes are scarce, and where bachelors are unpleasantly numerous."[15] The bachelors had the benefit of clean bedrooms, and the restaurant quickly made a reputation for good food. Hygiene was always a challenge in frontier restaurants, and Nellie was proud to claim that her kitchen had no cockroaches and that the flour was clean. For the opening in early October, four hundred guests were fed, which was a considerable feat for a new restaurant, especially from a kitchen without refrigeration beyond ice trucked into the town.

The Russ House menu was impressively large. Nellie's Sunday dinners, served at 4:30 PM, were so popular that she needed to bring in five extra waiters to help serve. On a typical winter Sunday guests were offered a choice of soups, baked salmon, braised ribs, roast lamb, veal, or pork. Desserts included plum pudding with hard sauce, followed by apples and walnuts. Another Sunday, diners had a choice of soups, trout, leg of mutton with caper sauce, lamb croquettes, and braised ham with champagne sauce, as well as an assortment of roasts. That Sunday, desserts included pumpkin and apple pie, jelly cake, and coconut pudding, followed by grapes, apples, and nuts. Nellie did much of the cooking, ably assisted by Sam Lee, her Chinese cook.

Nellie had a reputation as a good cook, but legend has the story of a diner who was dissatisfied with his dish of beans. As he complained, a lean, mustachioed fellow diner, said to be John "Doc" Holliday, came over to ask about the problem. Noticing his gun, the unhappy guest hastily decided the beans were the best he had ever eaten. Nellie was fortunate to have a defender in Doc; no one wanted him as an enemy. Wyatt Earp supposedly described his dentist friend as a man "whom necessity had made a gambler, a gentleman whom disease had made a frontier vagabond; a philosopher whom life had made a caustic wit; a long, lean ash-blond fellow nearly dead with consumption, and at the same time the most skillful gambler and the nerviest, speediest, deadliest man with a six-gun I ever knew." [16]

Somehow Nellie found time to continue fundraising for the Irish National Land League and for the Sisters of St. Joseph, her old friends from Tucson.

Since she had housed sick miners without charge at Russ House, the miners of the area were always sure to contribute when Nellie asked for donations. On the business and charitable front everything was going well, but Fanny was showing unmistakable signs of the disease that had killed her husband. Even Nellie could not manage Russ House, assist at the Delmonico, and care for her sister and the children. In mid-December the *Epitaph* announced that Nellie must sell her one-half interest in Russ House. "It is to be sold on account of a sister's sickness, which necessitates my entire attention elsewhere." [17] By year-end Fanny's business, the Delmonico, was listed for sale too. For a time Nellie devoted herself to her sister and the children, although she kept up her charitable work.

Outside town, rolling grassland and a growing population encouraged ranching, which was to play a significant role in the Tombstone story. Northern Mexico was cattle country, and raiding back and forth across the porous border had always been popular. In Arizona, the term "cowboy" came to mean outlaw. Gunmen ambushed the bullion stages coming from the silver mines and in most cases got away with it. In one ten-day period, the newspapers reported fourteen murders.

During this period of anarchy the town split into two factions. On one side were the rustlers and their protectors, the politicians who ran Cochise County. On the other were the officers, charged with enforcing federal laws such as those relating to mail robbery, and most of the town's merchants and miners, who just wanted to make a living. John Clum was one of the organizers of a vigilance committee to control lawlessness in Tombstone, a factor that helped him get elected mayor under the new city charter in 1881. Clum became a supporter of the Earp brothers.

Nellie continued to advertise in both of the town's rival newspapers, but her sympathies lay with her friend Clum and the merchants. The story of the October 1881 shootout at the O.K. Corral is part of the folklore of the Old West. Three rustlers died; Doc was shot in the back, though not seriously. Virgil and Morgan Earp had more dangerous wounds. Martial law was imposed and by November 1882, the streets of Tombstone were quiet again. The outlaw leaders were dead, mostly by violence, or had fled to Mexico.

While the factional hostility was rumbling below the surface, Tombstone stores continued to sell their wares, and restaurants were busy. Nellie bought and sold many mining claims in these years. Occasionally she bought alone, but she usually had partners, men she trusted from the Irish community. Her name was normally listed first on the legal documents, implying that she was the lead partner. Sometime after buying the claim she named in honour of Irish patriot Charles Stewart Parnell out in the Chiricahua Mountains, she purchased the Big Blue claim in the Huachuca Mountains. Other trades followed, and Nellie made money. She was solvent enough to continue wheeling and dealing, even after a disastrous prospecting expedition into Mexico. Her buy-in to the Big Commet claim near Tombstone dates from this period and was purchased for seven hundred dollars.

Fanny's tuberculosis went into remission for a while, encouraging her to think of working again. On Fremont Street, between Fourth and Fifth streets, she and Nellie found a suitable building and in late April of 1882 they opened a new hotel, The American. The dining room was large and served meals twenty-four hours a day to accommodate shift workers. The *Epitaph* extolled the restaurant's "elegant and elaborate style where customers would find meals as palatable as can be had in the city."[18] A June advertisement noted, "The hotel will be conducted in the same manner that has always characterized the hotels under their control, which is sufficient evidence that everything will be conducted in first class style."[19]

For a month everything went well, and then a fire, the second serious one in the town, started in a saloon on Allen Street and spread through the business sector. Friends of the Cashman sisters rallied to save The American by stationing themselves with buckets and dousing the building with water. They did save the building, but the women lost their clothing. Fanny's hair was singed, and Nellie sustained a nasty burn on one arm. However, knowing the fire hazard of the towns of the Old West, Nellie was insured. Damage to the hotel amounted to an estimated fifteen hundred dollars, but Nellie was insured for three thousand dollars and was able to recoup her losses. Within a few weeks The American was open for business again.

The fire was a setback for the town, as most of the business sector lay in ruins. Tombstone lost three of its premier hotels. The offices of the *Nugget* on Fourth Street were burned to the ground, which caused no sorrow among the supporters of the *Epitaph*, but Nellie's friend Clum was to lose his newspaper another way that year. He was unable to prevent the sale of the *Epitaph*, and its political affiliation changed from Republican to Democrat. On the surface, Tombstone was a bustling, lively community with two stable banks, schools, and a county hospital. A dozen big mines operated in the area, and there were many places where a tired miner could eat a good meal or lose some of his hard-earned money at faro or poker. The peak year for mine production was 1883, but there were problems ahead. The west was producing more silver than the Treasury could use, and some of the Tombstone silver ores were hard to process.

Joe Pascholy had backed out of the Russ House partnership to open his own new, large hotel. Nellie bought back in, which meant she was managing The American jointly with her sister as well as running Russ House. Her old grocery store appears to have been sold or leased to others by this point. Two hospitality businesses would have been work enough for most people, but at heart Nellie was a miner, and word of a promising gold placer strike on the Baja Peninsula of Mexico was too exciting to ignore.

Tombstone, 1881.
PHOTO BY C.S. FLY.

CHAPTER FIVE

BAJA AND TOMBSTONE

NELLIE HAD PROSPECTED for gold in the Cassiar and liked everything she knew about the metal. When news of the Baja discovery reached Tombstone in the spring of 1883, she invited men to join her, put together the outfit she would need, and was off on a stagecoach for the first part of the journey southwest. Months of superintending a kitchen behind her, Nellie was back in her mining clothes: trousers, shirt, and high boots. Among her companions were the owner of the Oriental Saloon, Milt Joyce, and Mark Smith, an attorney who later became an Arizona senator.

At Contention, west of Tombstone, they boarded a Southern Pacific Railroad train and travelled to the Mexican port of Guaymas on the Gulf of California. The line had been completed about a year earlier, and the journey from Tombstone took them only a day.

Guaymas had become the supply centre for the Baja gold rush, and there they bought burros and provisions. Nellie was named the leader of this group of twenty-one men. She was up to the task and assigned each man a responsibility: one to buy tools, another to obtain maps, another to make sure they had enough water. To reach Mulege on the Baja coast, they had to cross the gulf, a schooner journey that took four days. A smaller vessel then took them 100 miles (161 kilometres) up the coast to Trinidad Bay, from which the route led inland another 100 miles or so to the supposed goldfields.

Nellie decided that a reconnoitring party should go ahead, leaving the others to join them once they knew the worth of the placers. She and five or six of the men set off with burros; it was late May and they had underestimated the intense heat and aridity of the landscape. They thought they knew desert from Arizona, but conditions here were much harsher. Heat burned through the soles of their boots, and the horizon shimmered in waves. One of the party commented that not even a lizard could survive out there. Water quickly ran short. Before they reached the first waterhole, Nellie and her companions were in serious trouble. Moreover, prospectors returning to the coast reported that the best gold had gone, already mined by Mexicans and Yaqui Indians.

From here the facts of the fiasco are hazy. One rather unlikely legend has it that Nellie, setting off alone to seek water, met a priest who begged her not to reveal that there was gold in his parish for fear of disturbing the lives of his flock. John Clum said that Nellie told her nephew, Mike Cunningham, that, as party leader, she did indeed go to find water and that a good angel guided her to a Catholic mission out in the desert. Mexican parishioners helped her fill goatskins and load burros, and she got back to her companions, who were by now dangerously parched. No one died, but several had come close. In the same week two men from Europe died of thirst out in the desert. Nellie and her companions met up with the larger party and made it back to Trinidad Bay, where they rested and arranged a boat.

It was a story of danger and discouragement, and there was more to come. The captain of the ship that was to take them back to Guaymas was a hard-drinking man, and after they put to sea he appeared on deck in a wildly delusional state. Some of the prospectors tied him up and put him below deck to sleep it off, and sailors steered the boat back to Guaymas. Back on shore, prospectors and crew were arrested and thrown into prison for daring to take the captain prisoner. The jail was a filthy, evil-smelling place, and they were thankful to be rescued by the American consul, Alexander Willard, a few days later. The Baja California gold quest had been a memorably nasty experience, but Nellie's leadership was never in question. She was remembered as being a good sport and sharing the hardships cheerfully. The *San Diego Union* was fulsome in its praise of her ambitions and endurance. "In all the vicissitudes of life she has maintained the highest self respect . . . In Arizona she could raise a company at any time who would follow her to the death, either in search of gold or Apaches."[1]

The praise for her leadership was welcome, but the desert trip had affected Nellie's health, and in Tucson she sought help from a doctor, J.C. Handy, whom she trusted. Well again and back in Tombstone, chastened but not defeated, Nellie busied herself with her Russ House restaurant and helping out at her sister's boarding house. Fanny was frequently in bed, weary and coughing, and both women must have realized she had only a short time to live. Burdened by business cares and the children's needs, Nellie could not give her sister the specialized care she needed, so they made the painful decision to move Fanny to San Diego to be nursed by nuns. Fanny died in July 1884. Overnight, Nellie became the sole support not only of her mother but also of her sister's five children, ranging in age now from three to thirteen. Fortunately, Nellie was comfortably off in this period. She had income from Russ House and mining claims for collateral, and she had made several lucrative trades.

After her sister's death, Nellie and the young ones managed to fit into a small adobe house behind Russ House. In just three years the children had lost both parents and had had to leave their home in San Francisco. It was a huge dislocation, but the children adjusted to life with their aunt, who proved a firm but kind guardian.

The two older boys, Tom and Mike, could be mischievous. They would get into fist fights with school friends behind the house until Aunt Nell came out to separate the young combatants and then soothe injured feelings with slices of home-baked pie. Mike never forgot one potentially serious escapade. He and a friend both owned a burro, and one day when Aunt Nell was busy, they took off to the Dragoon

Mountains, pretending to be prospectors. It was a dangerous idea because the Apache were still strong in their mountain fastness. By evening the boys realized they had come a long way from town and were frightened. As Apache signal fires were lit in the mountains, the boys took refuge in an abandoned ranch house and huddled together in fear, hoping that if the Apache warriors swooped down they would not be discovered.

Fortunately for them, a prospector on his way into Tombstone had passed the boys trotting through the sagebrush toward the mountains, wondered what they were doing alone, and alerted Nellie. Without hesitation she found horses and a buggy, and set off in the dark. There were few ranches in Apache territory, and it wasn't hard for Nellie to trace the boys. Years later Mike admitted that they had been terrified and very relieved to hear his aunt calling to them. The following day Nellie sent a man out to retrieve the burros.

Nellie lived up to her obligations as a surrogate mother. For years she supported the children financially and saw that they got the best education she could manage, as well as a moral upbringing. For the kind of schooling that Tombstone could not offer, they were sent away to religious institutions, usually in

California. Mischievous Mike attended college in Los Angeles and Santa Fe. Working his way up through the ranks in Tombstone, he went on to become a prominent citizen of Cochise County. He named his eldest daughter Ellen in honour of his aunt. One of Nellie's two nieces became a nun, taking the name Sister St. Helena. They were all a tribute to Nellie's care.

Business and charitable endeavours had made Nellie a well-known figure in Tombstone, and in early 1884 she added to her legend with a quiet act of charity. The southern territory was shocked by an event known as the Bisbee massacre. It was a poorly executed robbery by five men who held up the Castaneda & Goldwater store in Bisbee. The town had no bank and the store acted in lieu of one, handling the payroll for the nearby Copper Queen mine. On the morning of December 8, 1883, the robbers rode into town. Two stayed on guard outside the store and three entered, to discover that the mine payroll had not arrived. Either angered or confused, the men took what they could from bystanders and the store safe. From there the robbery became a shooting spree; in the melee three people were killed and two wounded. The dead included a pregnant woman, struck by a stray bullet, and the deputy sheriff, who came running down the street at the sound of gunfire. Robbing bystanders as they went, the five rode out of town. Out in the desert they split the loot and separated.

Pursuit followed quickly. Sheriff Jerome L. Ward organized two posses. The Copper Queen mine posted handbills describing the wanted men, and a large reward was offered. Almost from the start, the sheriff and his new deputy, William Daniels, were suspicious of John Heath, a Bisbee saloon owner. Heath had been a cattle rustler in his youth and had a dubious reputation. However, Heath told the deputy that he knew the fugitives and asked to join a posse—a posse he was later found to have led astray.

Eventually all five outlaws were traced and arrested, although it took several weeks. Heath, now known to have masterminded the robbery, was tried separately. On February 20 he was convicted of second-degree murder and sentenced to life imprisonment. Although Heath had neither taken part in the robbery nor counselled violence, his sentence did not assuage local anger at the senseless shootings. A group of citizens from Bisbee and Tombstone broke into the county jail, captured Heath, and hanged him from a telegraph pole on Toughnut Street. A coroner's jury returned a verdict that could only have come from the Old West: "We the undersigned, a jury of inquest, find that John Heath came to his death from emphysema of the lungs—a disease common in high altitudes—which might have been caused by strangulation, self-inflicted or otherwise."[2]

The five men who had carried out the robbery were convicted of first-degree murder and sentenced to hang on March 28. Pleased with the successful outcome, Sheriff Ward sent out invitations to watch the execution from the jail yard, and a local businessman commissioned a carpenter to erect seating outside and started selling tickets. Nellie was horrified that the execution was turning into entertainment and begged the sheriff to have the bleachers pulled down. He declined to intervene, but the bleachers were dismantled the night before the execution by a group of miners. Nellie had a lot of influence with the miners, but it is not known if they were acting on her request. Though her nephew, Mike, said the destruction of the bleachers was done at his aunt's instigation, no contemporary newspaper gave her the credit.

What is known is that two and perhaps three of the men who were hanged that day were Irish and that Nellie had visited all of them in prison, along with two parish priests offering spiritual consolation. The *Tombstone Epitaph* reported that she was "in constant attendance" at the jail.[3] The men were depressed by a rumour that their bodies were to be handed over for dissection by medical students, and Nellie promised them she would see this did not happen. Their bodies were buried in the pioneer cemetery, the Boothill, and for the following ten nights two prospectors sent by Nellie slipped away from her restaurant with coffee pot, fry pan, and blankets to watch over the graves to prevent molestation. After ten days Nellie judged that citizens had lost interest in disinterring the men.

The Bisbee five were the first criminals to be legally hanged in Tombstone. The *Tombstone Republican*, a newspaper that existed for a short time only, stated that the men died well. Nellie and priests of the town had been with them all morning. According to John Clum, Nellie's spiritual support was persuasive enough to convert the three non-Catholics to her own faith in those last days.

Myth and fact can be hard to separate when a woman becomes a legend, but one story tells of Nellie's bravery: her role in saving the superintendent of the Grand Central Mining Company from mob violence. By 1884 metal prices were falling while mine workers were trying to get their labour conditions and pay improved. A Miners' Union strike brought out most of the men. According to the *Arizona Weekly Citizen*, union members took to the streets "exhibiting symptoms of a revengeful spirit." [4] E.B. Gage, the mine superintendent and a former leader of the vigilantes, was not a man easily intimidated, and he had kept the mines in full production by using scab labour. A crowd of union miners, perhaps as many as seventy men, headed toward the Grand Central mine. An altercation over wages resulted in the miners peppering the mine office with shot from pistols and rifles. A contingent from the army base at Fort Huachuca was brought in to maintain order. Perhaps fearing further violence, the Tombstone newspapers took the part of the mine owners.

Legend has it that, learning Gage was to be kidnapped and perhaps hanged by the miners, Nellie spirited him out of town, quietly taking him in her buggy and driving him south to Benson. At Benson, Gage took a train for Tucson and stayed away until the hotheads thought better of their plan. Mike Cunningham spoke of his aunt's adventure many times in later years, and John Clum believed it to be true. From a newspaper account, Gage was certainly absent from Tombstone for perhaps a week after the confrontation at the mine. Curiously, Nellie herself never spoke of saving Gage from harm. It could be that she did not wish to advertise her role for fear of alienating her many friends among the miners or that she simply was not given to publicizing her good deeds.

She and Gage remained friends, and at one time he invested in one of her mining claims.

Nellie worked on behind the scenes, keeping up her charitable work and influencing the political life of the town. She is said to have been responsible for the election of at least one city marshal. After the Tombstone hangings, the town became relatively quiet, but these were not propitious times for miners. Profits fell with the oversupply of silver. Then in 1886 water flooded mine shafts, an irony in the territory where water shortage had been the norm, and fire destroyed the pump houses and hoisting machinery at the Grand Central mine. The nearby Contention mine had pumps, but they were not large enough to keep it free of water. New pumps could have been purchased, but the falling price of silver made further salvage work pointless. The two mines were closed, and two-thirds of Tombstone's residents left town. Mining continued on a very minor scale, but the owners of the remaining mines found it more cost effective to have their ore shipped away for milling, resulting in a further loss of jobs.

Once Tombstone had been the largest city between San Antonio and the Pacific. Now it was dying. One after another Nellie's friends left town. John Clum settled in San Francisco for a while and then headed north in the Yukon gold rush. Wyatt Earp went on to speculate successfully in real estate in San Diego before he too moved north. Joe Pascholy, Nellie's oft-times partner and friend, explored opportunities around Yuma and then opened the Huachuca Hotel near the military fort, supplying beef from his ranch. Doc Holliday died of tuberculosis in 1895 after a last shot of whisky. Many of the minor outlaws from Tombstone later met violent deaths in gun duels.

After Fanny's death Nellie refurbished Russ House, promising that the restaurant would offer first-class food and service. At times, Arizona saw attempts to drive the Chinese out of employment and, despite the loyal service of her Chinese cook, Sam Lee, Nellie was not immune to racism. Her advertising stated that her waiters would come from eastern states and her cooks would be white men. Superintending her kitchen was a new chef, Benjamin Wurtmann, hired from California. In the winter of 1885 Nellie sold a property she owned along with two claims, the Grand Central South and the Southern Bell, to her friend Gage, the mining executive. She was paid six hundred dollars in gold coin. For a time Russ House was her only business interest. Over the years in which she was sole or part-owner, the boarding house–restaurant provided an income, a home, and a way to support her adopted family.

Woodcut of Kingston, New Mexico, in pioneer days,
by Howard Simon. Reproduced in *Black Range Tales*
by James A. McKenna, 1936 and 2002 editions.

CHAPTER SIX

RESTLESS FEET

WHILE NELLIE CONTINUED to run Russ House, she knew that the bonanza days of Tombstone were over and she needed a new and lucrative enterprise. Early in 1886, with a woman partner, Paulina Jones, an established restaurateur, Nellie moved to Nogales, Arizona, near the Mexican border. Nogales had been part of the United States since the Gadsen Purchase in the 1850s. Hot in summer and cold on winter nights, it was named for the walnut trees that grew in the passes connecting the small town with Mexico. Nogales showed promise of a worthwhile commercial future. It was a stop on the railroad between Tucson and the towns of Baja California, including the port of Guaymas in Mexico. Ranchers raised enough cattle to have to guard them from Apache raids. There was mining potential: silver and gold had been discovered, and a smelting works was nearing completion.

Nellie rented a building that had been a restaurant and opened her own restaurant and boarding house. Mrs. Jones took on the Palace Hotel and restaurant, which had fifty-two rooms. In less than three weeks Nellie had her new venture up and running, naming it once again the Delmonico, a name she believed always brought her success. The *Tombstone Epitaph* ran an advertisement, promising "The best table in the territory. Clean and comfortable beds. Bar supplied with the finest Liquors and Cigars."[1] Nellie was listed as manager of the Delmonico, and the proprietor was her nephew, T.J. Cunningham. Tom was only fifteen, but Nellie clearly wanted him to start earning and make his mark in the world.

The Delmonico had a short life. Not much more than three months after its opening the *Tombstone Epitaph* reported "Nellie Cashman has sold her hotel at Nogales."[2] Usually prescient about possibilities, Nellie had misjudged Nogales. No major mineral deposits were found. In time, agriculture and its location on the railroad between Tucson and the settlements of Sonora would pay off, but for the present Nogales was not worth investment.

Nellie had no time for vain regrets. Having found a buyer for the Delmonico she was off, first to visit her mother in San Francisco, and then on to another try in the territory. This time Nellie bought into the Palace Hotel in Tucson, not to own the hotel but to run the dining rooms. She was warmly welcomed. The town newspaper reported, "The public may expect a boom now, as Miss Nellie understands how to run a hotel."[3] But, like the Delmonico in Nogales, this was a short-lived enterprise. After life in Tombstone, Nellie found Tucson dull. Exploration took money and time, and mine development lay in the future. There could be no short-term gain. Nellie looked around.

She held on to a claim she owned with partners in the Tombstone area, but for the next decade she moved about. Newspaper reports spoke of her looking at claims in New Mexico, Idaho, Wyoming, and Montana. When she could, she sent for her sister's children during their school holidays. The younger Cunningham children grew up in institutions. It was not an ideal life, but Nellie was married to the mining world with its quick fluctuations of fortune. Russ House was the only semi-permanent home they had known, but Tombstone died and Nellie and the children had to move on.

In 1887 Nellie rode into Kingston, New Mexico, in the southwest of the territory. It was a dangerous land for pioneer prospectors. Quite apart from outlaws hiding in the desert country and willing to kill a prospector for his outfit, the Apaches were close to Kingston and had the latest firearms. Yet lucky strikes were made and many lead and silver mines were developed.

When Nellie arrived in Kingston, the camp was five years old and the hub of the whole area. A prospector named Jack Sheddon had discovered a rich vein of silver in the mountains, and his find triggered a small stampede. Sheddon's story is one of those improbable tales that enliven mining history. A bit of a ne'er-do-well and a drinker, Sheddon took himself out to the hills, probably to sleep off a hangover. Lying under pine trees, he woke to find his head resting on a rock that was almost pure silver. The rest is history. Never a large camp, Kingston was a wild place. Besides the mines and mills, in its heyday Kingston had twenty-two saloons, fourteen general stores, a dance hall, gambling halls, a brewery, and three newspapers. The community grew fast and attracted the usual hard-drinking mining fraternity, many of them Irish.

Nellie was a few years too late to be part of a memorable Christmas party, staged to support the opening of a new dance hall, the Casino. Everyone in town was invited and most came, including five colonels and their ladies, as well as local prostitutes and prospectors of assorted nationalities. Among the revellers was Ed Doheny, who would later become a household name as an oil magnate. In Kingston, Doheny was teaching school and unsuccessfully working a few claims he owned.

On the stagecoach coming into town a day or two earlier, a prospector and gambler called Johnny Roach made the acquaintance of a pretty girl from Denver and asked her to be his date for the party. He was having a bad run at the faro tables and drowned his sorrow to such effect that he sent word to his new friend to tell her he could not manage the party and she should stay away herself. But no pretty girl wants to spend Christmas Eve alone, and the hotel landlady found her a partner who was a good dancer. By midnight the two were cutting a rug on the fine new hardwood dance floor. Johnny meanwhile woke up, somewhat recovered from his hangover, and went to fetch his lady. Learning that she was already at the Casino with another man, he was furious and grabbed his Springfield rifle.

After breaking the glass door of the hall with the butt of his gun, Johnny shot out the lights.

In the melee that ensued, panicked guests rushed about in the dark. A colonel's dance partner known as Big Annie led a charge out through the back door of the hall. Unfortunately, the Casino was a split-level building, and Annie and others plunged thirty feet (nine metres) down into a creek. The only doctor was summoned and rushed in, adding to the confusion; arriving in the dark in his nightgown and without his usual wig, he was mistaken for a ghost. Gambler Johnny was arrested and spent a few hours in jail, but he was let out when he promised to pay for the damage at the Casino, as well as Big Annie's medical bill. Next day he was seen sharing an amicable Christmas meal with the girl from Denver.

Nellie opened a restaurant and boarding house named Cashman House, memorable because she may have employed Ed Doheny as a dishwasher. Some biographers have doubted Nellie's hiring of Doheny, but the dates of his sojourn in the town fit, and it is known that he was down on his luck and had a young wife to support. It may be that he took extra work until he could improve his lot. As an oil mogul he probably did not care to advertise the fact that he had once worked as a dishwasher. Nellie claimed he was good at his job.

Nellie settled in quickly and made friends. The camp was small, and she owned the best restaurant. A priest-historian, Father Francis Crocchiola, who wrote under the pseudonym F. Stanley about Kingston's early days, spoke of Nellie as the Florence Nightingale of the camp. As always she helped sick or out-of-luck miners, and when priests came to Kingston she rounded up the Catholics. Visiting priests must have been heartened by the robust attendance when they came to celebrate Mass.

Nellie was probably amused by the antics of four Irishmen known as the "four Neals," because they shared the same Christian name. The friends were good miners, but they had been activists who lost their jobs to scab labour in the coal mines of Pennsylvania. When Nellie knew them, the Neals were living rough in a camp of their own making a few miles from Kingston. There they located and mined a good silver prospect and could have made a fortune had they not shared a problem with alcohol as well as a first name.

They all loved wakes and funerals, and Neal O'Boyle managed to be a pallbearer at every Kingston funeral. He took the role seriously, dressing in a formal black suit, black gloves, stove-pipe hat, and polished shoes. At the bedside of the deceased he was known for his excessive compliments on the fine presentation of the corpse. Of course, liquid compensation was expected.

James McKenna, pioneer prospector and soldier of the southwest, related a story that speaks to Nellie's understanding of human frailty. "Nellie was an angel of mercy in Kingston," he wrote, "always on hand to care for the sick and to watch with the dead."[4] Nellie was praying alone by a corpse one day when Neal O'Boyle arrived, dressed and ready to give his usual theatrical performance. He asked Nellie for a drink, and she indicated a pitcher on the sideboard. O'Boyle gulped down a tumblerful and, forgetting the deceased, roared his dismay. If this belly-wash was alcohol, he claimed, it was fit only for Baptists. He begged Nellie to find him a drink strong enough to get him through the funeral. In the kitchen of the house she found a bottle of whisky kept for medicinal purposes, this being the home of teetotallers. Suitably fortified, O'Boyle set off for the funeral, telling Nellie she had saved his life but he would act no more as a pallbearer to Baptists.

But Kingston, like other camps, was hurt as the price of silver dropped. For Nellie, the camp did not fulfill its promise, and about fifteen months after arriving, she sold up and moved back to Tucson. She did not have long to ponder her next move. In 1888, in the Little Harquahala Mountains, northwest of Phoenix, three prospectors, including Mike Sullivan, struck the very rich gold ore body exploited as the Gold Eagle and Bonanza mines, the first of several major producers in those mountains. The ore lay in chimney veins, sometimes in solid nuggets of yellow gold as big as a man's fist. One nugget extracted from the quartz sold for ten thousand dollars.

The Spanish had known there were gold deposits in the mountains and so had the Tonto Apaches and Mexicans. A small but quite successful mine, the Socorro, was first worked in 1882, but nothing compared with the big strike and by December 1888 everyone knew about it. The gold was in quartz with significant iron content, meaning that machinery was needed to extract it. That required capital, but for those who could afford to get in on the ground floor, the prospects looked alluring.

Nellie liked to be early in on the mining scene, and prospectors were happy to see her ride into a new camp, believing she brought good luck. By Christmas she had bought provisions in San Francisco and Phoenix, and was heading out to the mountains. In San Francisco she was seen walking on Market Street by a Tucson acquaintance, Colonel

John Hull. Hull pointed her out to a correspondent for an English newspaper, the *London Story Paper*, and provided information about this rare female miner. According to the colonel, Nellie was the first woman going to the Harquahala camp. "American miners," he said, "had come to rely on her judgment about prospects and the worth of ores. Miners are superstitious, and they began to think that to have her around and get her good opinion would bring good luck. You can just bet she was treated like a Queen wherever she went."

Praising Nellie's adventurous spirit, the colonel added, "She no sooner hears of a new and promising camp than she starts for it. She buys town lots, placer sites, and lode claims for next to nothing and usually unloads at a big profit." Acknowledging that the mining world was one of boom and bust, the colonel noted that Nellie had been poor as many times as she had been rich. "She has big pluck though and if she goes broke in one place she soon makes a turn and gets up again. When she has a reverse she takes it nonchalantly, and is just as level-headed, self-contained and serene as if she had made a fortune." [5]

Toiling up the hill trail to Harquahala, Nellie was far from alone, even if she was the first woman to arrive. Teams of mules and wagons were streaming through the sagebrush, carrying prospectors who believed they were onto a good thing. A camp took root, starting from a store in a tent and a five-gallon jug of whisky. Nellie was pleased to see her old friend Wyatt Earp. He had been living in San Diego but, like Nellie, he could not resist the stories he had read of the big strike; he purchased roulette tables and alcohol, loaded mules, and headed out to open a saloon.

In the Mojave tongue, the mellifluous name Harquahala meant "running water high up" but, as in many camps, water was scarce. After a thirsty start for the camp, a pipeline was built to bring water twenty-one miles (thirty-four kilometres) from the mountains to a huge reservoir to supply the settlement and its forty-stamp mill. Timber was in short supply too and lumber, mostly Oregon pine, had to be freighted in from the coast and then moved overland from Yuma.

"High grading" has two meanings in the mining world. It means to extract only the best from an ore body, but it also means to conceal and steal away precious metals or gems. At Harquahala, Mexican labourers were brought in to do the heaviest work, at miserable pay. They were heavy pipe smokers, and it was a long while before the mine owners realized that they were sneaking out gold dust or small nuggets in the bowls of their pipes. White miners had their own ways to high grade. They would scrape for gold in the *arrastres*, a primitive device for crushing gold, masking the noise by having the camp children sing noisily to the accompaniment of the church's hand organ.

As mining camps go, Harquahala was not a riotous place but, since it had saloons but few or no places where a man could get a decent cooked meal, Nellie could have done well managing a kitchen. If she did open a restaurant, it may have been a minor pursuit. She bought claims, worked them, and made several trips to Phoenix to load up with supplies for resale to the prospectors. She was far from poor at this time. Heading to church in Phoenix, she realized she had dropped her purse containing four hundred dollars. Young boys found the purse and their father made sure it was returned to Nellie. At that time four hundred dollars was a handsome sum of money.

Was Harquahala the scene of the only romance of Nellie's life? Rumours circulated in the camp that she and Mike Sullivan were to marry. Sullivan was now a wealthy man. He and Nellie were both prominent citizens, both Irish Catholics, and they shared a passion for mining. The *Phoenix Daily Herald* of February 23, 1889, stated that Sullivan and Miss Cashman were on their way to find a priest to officiate at their wedding. If there was any truth to the rumour, the affair was short-lived. In her heart Nellie must have known she was not cut out for the constraints of marriage. Sullivan sold out, partially to a San Francisco syndicate, and returned east. He and Nellie did not meet again.

Though self-taught, over the years Nellie had developed an impressive knowledge of mining geology. She was sufficiently respected that the *Arizona Daily Star*, in March 1889, published her analysis of the workings and prospects of the principal Harquahala mines after a four-day tour. At Mine No. 3, owned by Sullivan and his two partners, a shaft had been sunk twenty feet (six metres) down. The plan was to continue to fifty or sixty feet (fifteen to eighteen metres) "and see by drifting [i.e. tunnelling out sideways from the main shaft] if there are any walls, for this is the finest and largest ledge of exceedingly rich gold ore I have ever seen and if it should hold out to proposed depth this mine alone will make as good a mining town as Tombstone or Bodie [California] ever made."[6]

Since Nellie had a claim near Mine No. 3 she was naturally anxious to see development, but the report is convincing for its grasp of geological details, and she discusses like a professional the mining methods and equipment being used.

For Harquahala to turn into a bonanza, big capital

investment was needed. This would take time. Nellie's philosophy was to stay with good claims but move on when they did not give quick returns. Harquahala did not work out quite as she had hoped, and there was no point in staying. Like Wyatt Earp, and Sullivan and his partners, Nellie packed her bags. When she sold her claims she probably did very well. Her prize claim lay close to the original strike and near some of the richest in the area. By late spring 1889 Nellie was gone, back to Tucson where, according to the *Arizona Gazette* she needed to recuperate from an illness.

After that, Nellie moved about like a gypsy; her movements are hard to track. She explored opportunities in Prescott in northwest Arizona, where there had been new gold finds, but seems to have stayed only weeks. In those nomadic years she traded claims on behalf of Fanny's children, and at times Mike, clearly her favourite, travelled with her. He later recalled prospecting in Idaho, Wyoming, and Montana. He remembered living in a cabin with the snow piled up 9 feet (2.7 metres) high outside. Winter or not, his aunt set a fast pace, and Mike found he could not keep up. "We were always on the move," he told a newspaper reporter, "looking for gold and silver."[7]

Toward the end of 1889 the *Arizona Daily Star* reported that Nellie had just returned from South

Africa and was back to recruit local men to explore a hitherto unknown diamond region. Nellie stated that she wanted men from Arizona because "men here are more reliable, courageous, and can endure more hardships than any she has met in her travels."[8] It is a warm accolade for the kind of prospectors she had known over the years, but the story raises questions. Did she make the trip to South Africa? Five or six months of her life at that time are unaccounted for, so the journey is possible. It seems unlikely that she would have allowed the newspaper report if it were untrue, and yet it supposes a very hurried journey in the age of sailing ships. Landing in Cape Town, capital of the British Cape Colony, after several weeks at sea, Nellie would have faced an inland journey of more than 495 miles (nearly 800 kilometres) to the Kimberley diamond fields of the Northern Cape. Many travellers would have made the journey with oxen and a wagon, but Nellie was a good horsewoman and she may have ridden all or most of the way. A year later a rail link opened between Cape Town and Bloemfontein, 93 miles (150 kilometres) from Kimberley, but Nellie was a year too soon for such comfort. Along the banks of the Orange River, she would have joined thousands of prospectors digging with picks and shovels and sifting through soil in a desperate attempt to emulate the young Boer boy who had stumbled on the first of the legendary diamonds without even trying.

Living conditions were harsh, and soon there were huge logistical problems of separating individual claims as diggers turned a hillside into a giant hole. Many were glad to sell out to wealthier men like Cecil Rhodes, who bought up a number of small mines to set up his company, De Beers. As so often happened in mining, fortunes were made not from the ores but from ancillary businesses. Rhodes made his first fortune renting water pumps to the miners.

Meanwhile, overproduction caused a drop in the price of diamonds. Nellie was by no means poor at this stage of her life, but she was facing industrial-scale mining. Apparently she returned to Arizona to try to drum up financial backing; she did not manage that and never returned to South Africa.

In 1895 Nellie decided to take a vacation. Apart from family visits, this may have been the first of her life. She sailed to Juneau, Alaska, a gold-mining camp picturesquely situated between water and mountains. As the eagle flies, it was only 200 miles (322 kilometres) from her old home in the Cassiar district, but no roads led in or out of Juneau. In this small waterfront community, Nellie met up with miners she had known in the Cassiar. Round a campfire they swapped stories of the old days, and Nellie was glad to find that she was remembered with respect and affection. Like them, Nellie believed the north country would yet prove the richest for gold, but she was involved in a number of claims in western camps and did not think she could pull up stakes quickly. Some of her old miner friends took their quest north and Nellie went back to Arizona.

For a few months Nellie moved about, investigating prospects in Sonora, Mexico, and Colorado, where she encountered old friends from Tombstone such as the Earp brothers. But the Minas Prietas gold property in Mexico was a huge, industrial-scale operation, and in Colorado she had missed the right time to buy into the Cripple Creek rush. A rich gold-bearing ore had been discovered in 1890 high on the southwest slopes of Pike's Peak in the Colorado Rockies, sparking one of the largest gold stampedes in mining history. The population jumped from five hundred to ten thousand in three years, and five mines went into production in Cripple Creek and the neighbouring camp of Victor. But the good claims had been filed before Nellie rode up the steep mountain trail, and an ugly miners' strike in 1894 poisoned the camp atmosphere.

Wasting no time on regrets, Nellie mounted her

horse and rode south to Tucson, covering the distance of 66 miles (106 kilometres) from Casa Grande to Tucson in one ride. She was still newsworthy in Tucson. The *Arizona Daily Star* of October 24, 1895, announced the arrival of "one of the most extraordinary women in America, Nellie Cashman, whose name and face have been familiar in every important mining camp or district on the coast for more than twenty years." For this tough woman the long horseback ride had been no problem although "it was a jaunt that would have nearly prostrated the average man with fatigue. She showed no sign of weariness, but went about town in that calm businesslike manner that belongs particularly to her." [9] The story was picked up by the *Los Angeles Times*, which noted, "When in camp, and she has been continuously in camp, she has lived a miner's life and has always enjoyed the deepest respect of the men with whom she has been associated." [10]

Nellie's wanderings can be hard to follow because she made so many moves. Early in 1896 she reappeared in Globe, first a silver- and later a copper-mining town, 80 miles (128 kilometres) east of Phoenix. The rough little town supposedly acquired its name from a globe-shaped piece of silver found by an early prospector. Situated in scenic mountain and forest country, Globe was a tough place, noted for murders and stagecoach robberies. It was also in Apache territory, but an arbitrary move by the secretary of the interior removed the mineral region from the San Carlos Apache Reservation. New silver discoveries prompted an inflow of prospectors, and by the summer of 1876, Globe had an official townsite and elected officials. Silver mining was phased out by 1890 with the market glut, but copper finds led to big business. Two companies, the Old Dominion and United Globe, employed hundreds of men, and United ran a smelter at Buffalo, a mile (1.6 kilometres) from town.

It looked promising, and Nellie arranged to take over management of the Buffalo Hotel and Restaurant near the smelter. Advertisements in February editions of the *Arizona Silver Belt* announced that she was open for business and promised, "the table of excellent quality . . . lunches a specialty." [11] Globe was an isolated camp, but Nellie was an old hand at managing supplies.

However, this was not to be a profitable enterprise. In a matter of months, the mining business in Globe collapsed. The price of copper fell, while costs were high because the ore had to be packed out across 120 miles (193 kilometres) of desert to reach the nearest railhead—a situation improved when the first train reached Globe in the winter of 1898. In the slump, the Buffalo smelter closed, and both the Old Dominion and United Globe companies saw their profits plummet. The *Silver Belt* noted that many of the miners and mill workers left debts behind when they gave up on Globe. Restaurants, stores, and saloons suffered during the exodus. Nellie hung on for a while, but with business dwindling, it was pointless. Once again involved in a property deal, she managed to sell out. At times, buying and selling must have been exhausting. Perhaps the legalities were simpler then, and some deals may have been settled with a handshake. Although Nellie would take on a lawsuit if she thought it justified, she had the reputation of being an honest woman.

Nellie was now fifty-one. She had made money over the years, but she had given a lot away and educated her sister's children. She needed success. Her search for the elusive bonanza strike was becoming frantic. In July 1897, she moved on, this time far west to Yuma on the Colorado River. Yuma was never a mining camp, but it offered opportunities for entrepreneurs. Spanish military expeditions in the sixteenth century had passed this way and realized that a point north of the present town was the ideal site for a post. Here the broad river was scarcely 1,000 feet (305 metres) across. As time passed, a rope crossing was replaced by a ferry, and from the mid-nineteenth century, the Yuma Crossing was the main steamboat stop on the Colorado. Cargo moving on the river was chiefly related to mines and military outposts. Thousands of stampeders passed through Yuma in the 1849 gold rush to California. After Arizona separated from New Mexico Territory in 1863, Yuma became the county seat for the area. The Southern Pacific Railroad reached this corner of the southwest in 1877, adding a railroad bridge over the river. Nellie arrived in Yuma in the searing heat of summer, but by now she was used to extremes of temperature, and she was not one to complain. With cool nights and a lack of humidity, most people found the subtropical desert climate healthy.

In Yuma Nellie opened yet another hotel, little knowing that her world was to change dramatically. She took over the Jones Hotel, renamed it the Hotel Cashman, and arranged for cooks and supplies, and soon after arriving she was advertising in the *Arizona Sentinel*, "table unsurpassed, charges reasonable"[12] Meals would be offered on the European and American plans. As a further inducement, the hotel offered a first-class bar.

The *Sentinel* welcomed Nellie's new venture, describing her as one who had conducted similar hotels and restaurants in every mining camp in the west and a woman who intended to give the public first-class service in every particular. In Yuma Nellie was joined by a niece, Mamie Cunningham. For Mamie it was a fortunate step. She fell in love with Miles Archibald, a guard at the Yuma Territorial Prison, and the pair married.

The hotel was running well when news of the sensational discoveries in the Klondike reached Arizona. Nellie quickly forgot the quieter prospects of Yuma and tried to extricate herself from her hotel. She also tried to find a backer who would risk five thousand dollars to send her north with six experienced prospectors. As with the South African venture, she did not find men to accompany her, and another attempt in Tucson was also unsuccessful. After her death it was said that her nephew, Mike, had put up some money. Nellie had done well in Harquahala but not from mining and, although she was respected, her twenty years in the southwest had kept her on the move without a major mining triumph. Undeterred, Nellie decided to set out for the Yukon alone.

No miner of her experience and reputation could resist the siren call of a truly colossal gold find. Clarence Berry, a spectacularly successful Klondike miner, came back to California to tell the world,

"Two million dollars taken from the Klondike region in less than five months, and a hundred times that amount waiting for those who can handle a pick and shovel."[13] Berry made it sound extraordinarily easy. Of course, it wasn't, as many were to find out. Fired with optimism, the stampeders set out from farms, stores, and mining camps all over the continent. They did not care who had first discovered the gold in the Klondike valley. Maybe that honour was due the taciturn Canadian Robert Henderson, or maybe the significant prospector in the Klondike story was the cheerful Californian George Carmack, and his Tagish Indian wife and brothers-in-law. It mattered little to rushers from "Outside" so long as they could claim their share of the gold.

Nellie left Arizona with the good wishes of most people whose lives she had touched. Several newspapers, including the *Tombstone Prospector*, reported her departure, saying, "Miss Nellie Cashman, one of the most favourably known women in Arizona, arrived from Yuma yesterday. Miss Nellie is preparing to organize a company for gold mining in Alaska, where she has visited three times. Her many friends in Arizona will wish her success, for during her twenty years residence in the territory she has made several fortunes, all of which have gone for charity."[14]

Dyea Beach, Alaska, 1897.
IMAGE D-04430 COURTESY OF ROYAL BC MUSEUM AND ARCHIVES.

CHAPTER SEVEN

THE KLONDIKE TRAIL

B Y MID-FEBRUARY 1898 Nellie was in Victoria, outfitting for the Klondike. Though proudly American, Nellie thought she got better deals buying supplies in Victoria. The town was home to her good friends, the Sisters of St. Ann, and Nellie was always happy to see what progress had been made to the hospital she had helped to finance. The sisters had an eager interest in news from the north, knowing they were needed as nurses in a booming frontier community. Bishop Fabré of Montreal had advised the Mother House in Quebec to send St. Ann nuns to serve in the Yukon, and three sisters had been chosen. The order already had a presence in Alaska, with teaching missions in Juneau and, more recently, at Holy Cross on the Lower Yukon River and, for a time, Akulurak, on the Bering Sea.

In the waning years of the century, Victoria was a growing town of nearly 20,000 people. The Klondike quest saw a repetition of the Fraser River gold rush madness. Stampeders were mainly American. Tents of all kinds sprouted along the streets near the harbour. Hard bargaining ensued for horses, dogs, and suitable clothing. The gold seekers also needed tents and stoves and basic mining equipment. Foodstuffs had to be purchased too, enough to take each traveller through a winter in a distant settlement 600 miles (966 kilometres) from the coast. The usual supplies were flour, slab bacon, dried beef, rolled oats, dried fruits, and potatoes, butter in cans, alcohol, coffee, tea, and sugar. Wise travellers, or more probably the better outfitting merchants, knew that food, clothing, and utensils all had to be double-packed in stout canvas bags and then repacked in sacks that could be managed by one person.

All the Pacific ports were competing for business. Victoria did well from the Klondike rush, offering goods at prices below the Seattle norm, with the additional advantage that stampeders would not have to pay duty on them as they crossed the passes into Canada. Wearing apparel was exempt from customs duty but other goods were not. This was a cost that Seattle merchants tried to hide from customers.

While outfitting, the stampeders were vying for places on ships headed to Dyea and Skagway, the starting-off points for the two passes through the mountains separating the coast from the Yukon. Many of the ships were unfit for service on a route that took passengers out from the relative safety of the Inside Passage into open water with few navigation aids. Not only were many of the ships unseaworthy, they were all overloaded with prospectors, horses, mules, and dogs.

Even with the local excitement, not to mention the boost to the economy, Nellie's arrival from San Francisco was noteworthy in Victoria. She stayed at Burnes House near the harbour, an impressive hotel built by an Irishman, Tommy Burnes. Miners she had known in the Cassiar, now settled in Victoria, came round to shake her hand and talk about the old days. A reporter for the *Victoria Daily Colonist* was sent to the hotel, and the paper ran his interview under the heading "Miss Nellie Cashman the first white woman in Cassiar's mines visits Victoria." The story ran, "She is out now for a big stake, nothing more or less than the motherlode of the far-famed Klondike region. She says if her experience in quartz mining will stand her in good need and her proverbial good luck in mining matters stays with her, she will have a chance at least to stake out a few claims in the mountains of gold which is thought to enrich all the north."

Nellie encouraged the reporter to ask how she would dress on the expedition and answered her own question, telling him, "Well, in many respects as a man does, with long heavy trousers and rubber boots. Of course when associating with strangers, I wear a long rubber coat. Skirts are out of the question up north, as many women will find out before they reach the gold fields." The reporter commented, "Miss Cashman is a lithe, active looking woman with jet black hair, and possesses all the vivacity and enthusiasm of a young girl. Her personality is very striking."[1] It was a pleasing tribute. Nellie was fifty-three now and had put on weight, but her sense of adventure had not dimmed with the years.

Victoria was buzzing with rumours of the looming war between the United States and Spain. The cause was the independence of Cuba and Puerto Rico, Spain's last colonies in the New World, and the promotion of American interests in those islands. Nellie thought of Ireland and saw a David and Goliath

struggle against oppression and wrongful posses-
sion. She decided to continue north but, should war
be declared, she was ready to return to Nevada to
organize a company of women to join the fight. She
declared, "I do not value all the gold in Klondike as
much as I would a chance to fight those treacherous
Spaniards."[2] It sounded like wild talk, but it was
sincere. Twenty years later she actually did organize
a company of young men and set off at their head
prepared to fight in the First World War.

Nellie expected to take on the Klondike in the
company of her nephew, Tom, and another young
man. They were the right age and ready for adventure. Tom had saved some money and told her he
wanted to go. They were to have met in San Francisco
but Tom was not there, nor waiting in Victoria. She
believed he might have gone ahead to Wrangell, and
she wanted to leave the final decision on the route
they would take to the goldfields until they met up.
In Victoria she had the odd experience of encounter-
ing an imposter. She had sent ten dollars and a letter
to a merchant she knew in Seattle, asking him to keep
a lookout for Tom Cunningham. A young man of the
same name appeared in Victoria, representing himself
as her nephew. It was some while since Nellie had
seen the real Tom, but she was not fooled for long.

With characteristic generosity, she allowed the fake nephew to keep the dollar he had left over from her gift; it would keep him going in meals for a few days. Nellie could have had him arrested.

A happier meeting in Victoria was with the chief justice of the province, the Honourable Theodore Davie. Nellie had first met him after the Cassiar rescue, and he was pleased to see her again. Writing to her after their meeting Davie said, "I have no doubt that the unflinching courage and determination which have been yours in the past years, will likewise guide you to success and fortune in the perilous trip to the Yukon, which, in mid-winter you are about to take." [3]

Nellie had an advantage over many of the stampeders crowding the wharves: she knew what conditions would be like in the north. Two years before, she had travelled to Alaska with companions investigating placer prospects, but they were poorly provisioned and had to turn back as winter set in. She had made the memorable rescue journey in the Cassiar in bitter winter weather, and there she had learned to use snowshoes. She had lived in mining camps for most of the past twenty-six years, and experience had honed in her a sound instinct for promising ore beds. Last but not least, despite trying to raise funds from backers, Nellie still had money. She would be able to buy claims and, if necessary, hire men to work them for her. And if fortune eluded her in the goldfields, she could fall back on her experience managing restaurants. How well Nellie knew that tired prospectors did not want to cook for themselves at the end of the day.

All these factors set Nellie apart from most of her fellow gold seekers. Many of the Klondike hopefuls were urban men, clerks and storekeepers, totally unprepared for the hard physical work, the food shortages, and the harsh winters of the north. These innocents, who believed they could make a quick fortune in the north, were known as "cheechakos," a corruption of a term used by the Native peoples to differentiate them from the "sourdoughs," men and women who had survived at least one winter in the north. Women too were caught up in the Klondike fever but were outnumbered nine or ten to one. A few were wives and one or two were widows, but most were entertainers, singers, and dancers, and, of course, prostitutes. People set off by the thousands, with painfully little idea of what lay ahead. Better prepared were the experienced miners, men who had worked in the camps of California, Colorado, and Montana, but they were in a minority. Far too many of the stampeders were neophytes, and misinformation about the Yukon was widespread. Journalists who had never left Chicago or San Francisco were ready to pen illusory stories of adventure rewarded by wealth, stories that gave no idea of the dangers involved.

Determined to avert needless tragedy, the North-West Mounted Police, assisted by the career soldiers of the Yukon Field Force, enforced a ruling forbidding stampeders to enter the Canadian Yukon without a year's supply of provisions—about 900 pounds (408 kilograms) of food, exclusive of tea and coffee. Men who knew the north approved. Stepping off the steamer *City of Topeka* in Victoria in January 1898, Fred Berry, a brother of the highly successful Klondike miner-prospector Clarence Berry, told the press, "People seem to imagine that when they reach Dawson their troubles are over but I can assure you they only then begin. Don't misunderstand me, I am not running down the Yukon; for, on the contrary, I consider it a splendid country, with great riches in quartz mines as well as the placer; but the country is a very rough and difficult one to travel over, and one has to endure the greatest hardships in prospecting. Consequently, only those who are well supplied can hope to do well."[4]

Like all the stampeders, Nellie was turning over in her mind which of several routes to take. She had to rule out the all-water journey, from Seattle to the port of St. Michael on the Bering Sea and thence up the Yukon River on smaller vessels. It might sound the route of least effort, but it was a 4,000-mile (6,437-kilometre) journey and possible for only a few weeks in summer. Nellie's first choice was to follow the Stikine River through the Cassiar district and then trek overland the 850 miles (1,368 kilometres) to Dawson. She left Victoria on March 9 on the ss *Centennial* and four days later reached Wrangell.

Tom was not waiting for Nellie at Wrangell, and there was another disappointment. Travellers returning from the interior reported that because of a mild winter, the surface ice of the Stikine was slush, making travel with a laden sled virtually impossible. That left Nellie with a choice of two trails in from the coast—from Skagway, a lawless town that led to the White Pass, or from Dyea, some miles farther up the narrow and windy fiord known as the Lynn Canal, the starting point for the Chilkoot Trail. The two routes ran almost parallel and merged inland.

Both routes were formidable. Looking up from the tent town of Dyea, the Chilkoot summit might or might not be visible; it was often lost in mists. It was 17 miles (27 kilometres) from Dyea but it lay 3,500 feet (1,067 metres) above the shoreline.

Sometimes the summit was inaccessible for days because of blizzards, and then, not even the Chilkat Tlingit packers would travel. The trail through the gap was so steep that at one point, known as The Scales, men and women had to climb one thousand steps cut in the ice. It was a congested and gruelling climb.

The White Pass route was 10 miles (16 kilometres) longer but the summit, 20 miles (32 kilometres) from Skagway, was more than 600 feet (183 metres) lower than the Chilkoot Pass, making for a more gradual ascent. It was still an arduous climb, remembered for the cold, the boulders, the streams, and the mud of spring and summer. Even in late May the temperature on the mountains could be minus 5°F (-20°C). Pack animals were forced along the trail and perhaps as many as three thousand horses and oxen died, victims of overloading, neglect, or lack of forage.

John Clum regretted that Nellie in later years did not reminisce, at least for the record, about her route to Dawson. It was a journey no one could forget, but for Nellie it may have been simply one more hazard-ous expedition in a challenging life. It seems most probable that she chose the perilous Chilkoot Trail. She travelled in winter, when the ice steps made the ascent slightly easier than the soft slush and mud of summer. At the Chilkoot Pass, prospectors entered Canadian territory, and Americans, by far the majority, were irked at having to pay duty on the goods they had hauled up the Alaskan side. Nellie paid no duty on the outfit she had purchased in Victoria, but it fell short of the stipulated weight; apparently she charmed her way through the different police checkpoints. Gold seekers who adhered to the supplies stipulation had to make perhaps twelve round trips of 52 miles (84 kilometres) to carry and cache their goods near the summit, slide back down the mountain, retrieve another pack, and begin the laborious ascent again and again. After the summit came the descent, down through spindly pine trees where stampeders with aching muscles stumbled over tree roots. It could take two months or more to complete the Chilkoot Trail.

On the eastern side of the passes lay the network of lakes leading to the headwaters of the Yukon, the mighty river that emptied into the Bering Sea 3,000 miles (4,828 kilometres) away. The river was gripped by ice until mid- or late May each year, meaning that stampeders either continued on foot or camped by the lakes while they built a boat to carry them north at spring thaw. By the time the river was navigable, the shores of Lakes Bennett and

Lindeman were crammed with rafts, scows, skiffs, and canoes, some barely serviceable. Building a boat was not easy without experience. The obituary tribute in the *British Daily Colonist* quotes Nellie speaking of building a boat.[5] Presumably she paid for help.

From the lakes, it was a 500-mile (805-kilometre) journey down the Yukon River to the goldfields. South of Whitehorse lay the whirlpool of Miles Canyon and the Whitehorse Rapids with its submerged rocks. Many boats were wrecked there, swamped by waves or shattered by the rocks. Women and children had been ordered by the North-West Mounted Police to climb the river banks and hike round the dangers of the rapids, but Nellie recalled for her journalist friend, Fred Lockley, "going through the White Horse rapids, Five Finger rapids and all the others. Believe me, it's some journey, all right, to go through these rapids. I never want to travel any faster than I did there."[6]

Ten miles (sixteen kilometres) beyond Whitehorse lay Lake Laberge, thirty-one miles (fifty kilometres) in length. Here Nellie was overtaken by a young American prospector, Edward Morgan, and his Australian partner. Through a ghostwriter, Morgan later chronicled the adventures of his two years in the Klondike in a book aptly titled *God's Loaded Dice*. Morgan's description of his encounter with Nellie is convincing, but there is no accounting for the date he gives of 1897. Perhaps in later years Morgan's memory played him false, or possibly he wanted to be remembered as one of the earliest stampeders into the Klondike. He spoke admiringly of Nellie as "a lone, undaunted figure in the wilderness." Although the lake ice was smooth, the weather was bitterly cold, and they had all been travelling for days in minus 32°F (-35°C) temperatures. Morgan told his biographer, "We overtook a prospector struggling forward with a small, but heavily loaded sled, drawn by the voyager and a lone dog, of no great size or strength. Between them they were not making much progress and we readily granted permission to the traveler to hook on to the rear of our sleds for a lift for the next half-dozen miles or so."

The two men were surprised to find they had offered help to a woman. She was, Morgan noted, "a rather undersized figure, attired in mackinaw coat and trousers, with the regulation heavy boots and fur-lined cap."[7] Nellie was suitably dressed but had only one dog, while most of the stampeders who could afford dogs travelled with several. When it came time to camp for the night, Morgan's partner, a taciturn fellow, refused to allow a woman to camp with them. Given Nellie's age it was an odd stance, but after a shared supper she camped away from them and travelled on alone. Morgan had enjoyed her company and could well believe she had talked her way past the Mounties. They were to meet many times in Dawson.

Nellie seems to have reached Dawson in the spring of 1898, ahead of the great inrush of stampeders who were waiting at the lakes for spring breakup. She must have made the decision to press ahead on foot along the frozen river with her loaded sled and one small dog. Nellie knew how to camp in winter, but there were many obstacles and dangers for travellers. They faced frostbite, snow blindness, and the exhaustion of stumbling on day after day in the near-perpetual darkness of the northern winter. Without reliable maps, stampeders could only guess that following the Yukon River would bring them to Dawson. By the time Nellie reached the Stewart River, where it empties into the Yukon, the days were noticeably longer, a welcome change from the long darkness. At the confluence of the Yukon and Klondike rivers, the settlement suddenly appeared beyond a rocky bluff. Spread along the bank at the foot of a scarred mountain lay a motley collection of tents, shacks, saloons, and stores. For now, it was journey's end for Nellie.

Fewer than half of the hundred thousand gold seekers who set out actually reached Dawson, and very few found the gold they believed would be there for the taking. The Klondike story is full of ironies. By the time the main wave of men and women arrived, the best claims had been staked. In the weeks that followed, the shoreline was full of outfits men were trying to sell off to enable them to pay for their passage home. Sometimes gold was found by cheechakos in unlikely places, defying the experience of veteran miners. The winter of 1897 was memorable: the camp was awash in gold dust and nuggets but so short of food that there was very little to buy at any price.

And yet the north cast its spell. While some partnerships ruptured on the trail or in the stifling winter cabins, many lifelong friendships were forged. Nothing in later life could compare with the experience the gold seekers had shared. Some men, who left the Klondike with money, tried life on the Outside and returned. Father William Judge, the much-loved priest of the northern missions, commented in a letter from Nulato, Alaska, "There seems to be something about this country that fascinates all who come here, for I have never yet met one, even of those who come to make money, who wished to leave it as long as he could get something to do."[8]

Dawson, Yukon Territory, 1899.
IMAGE B-06746 COURTESY OF ROYAL BC MUSEUM AND ARCHIVES.

CHAPTER EIGHT

DAWSON

DAWSON HAD A strategic location and the land was flat, but it was swampy and prone to flooding after the river ice broke up. However, the creeks and hills near Dawson yielded the gold that lured prospectors to the Klondike, so the town is remembered as the setting of the world's most memorable gold rush. Soon tents and cabins spread for miles along the river banks, with little space for newcomers. Some prospectors settled in Klondike City, better known as Lousetown, an old Indian salmon-fishing camp across the river.

Dawson owed its existence to a trader, Joe Ladue,

who had moved fast on hearing of Carmack's strike. Ladue recognized an opportunity; he rafted his sawmill to Dawson, laid out a townsite, and began selling lots. Within a year they commanded exorbitant prices.

When Nellie arrived, apparently in late April 1898, Dawson was low on food, the mosquitoes were bad, and the centre of town was awash in flood water. Many stampeders who had travelled light and fast through the passes in the fall of 1897 had come without adequate provisions, believing that with the fortune they intended to make, they could buy anything they needed. The two trading companies of the Klondike, the Alaska Commercial Company and the North American Transportation and Trading Company, knew better, and the head of the North-West Mounted Police gave orders that a thousand people must leave the town. Offered free passage, some left on the last steamship. Others, in boats they owned, tried to reach trading posts to the south before they were frozen in. The temperature was minus 50°F (-45°C) for days on end, and some people died in the attempt.

Their departure left about 2,000 men and 120 women in Dawson, while 4,000 to 5,000 people toiled at their diggings along the creeks. No one actually starved, but it was a lean winter, with scurvy the painful reality for some. Gold was plentiful, whisky and cigars were available, but the few restaurants ran short on staples, the beans, bacon, dried potatoes, apples, and coffee that made up the stampeder diet. Food costs were high. Potatoes, prized because they warded off scurvy, sold for a dollar each. Tallow candles, another prize for a dingy cabin, sold for up to two dollars and fifty cents each. Coal oil and kerosene for lamps had become almost unobtainable at any price.

Out on the creeks, work continued, despite the bitter temperatures. Moving supplies by dogsled was easier in winter, and it was possible to sink and work shafts without fear of flooding or cave-in. Men lit fires to soften the frozen ground, which allowed them to dig. Inside the shaft, usually about 6 feet (1.83 metres) square, one man shovelled soil and gravel into a bucket while his partner worked the windlass above, hauling up the buckets. Jeremiah Lynch, an American senator who spent three years in the Klondike, commented, "It seemed pitiful to see a man standing on the frail platform, slowly turning the tedious windlass in a keen, biting atmosphere 45 degrees below zero."[1] As the shafts deepened, work slowed because the poisonous gases from the fires had to disperse before the miners could safely climb down. If the mine looked promising, the next stage was to follow the veins of rock, sending tunnels, or drifts, out from the shaft. The rubble was piled up near the digging, waiting for the spring thaw that sent water gushing down the hillsides and let the miners move on to sluicing.

Lynch claimed that when he met miners a year after they had first come to the Klondike, they looked greatly improved in health, fit from hard work in the champagne air of the hills. He must have meant when smoke from smouldering fires was not trapped by the fogs of autumn. Some men may have been fit, but Lynch had the advantage of money and could afford the best food Dawson could offer. To be fair, he fed his own workers well. At one point he had a hundred men working at his mine. They toiled a twelve-hour day and were paid fifteen dollars. It was far more than they could have earned in the south and, even allowing for the high cost of living in Dawson, a frugal man who kept away from the girls and the bars could probably save half his wages. Much depended on health. Miners who did not strike gold and ate poorly often climbed out of their shafts sick with bronchitis or even tuberculosis. And it was all a gamble. Weeks melted away as shafts were dug, but often the effort was wasted and no gold was found at bedrock.

By 1900 steam, forced through a nozzle, was being used at most of the diggings to blast away gravel and thaw the dirt. It was much faster than the old smouldering fire method, but the boilers that were needed to heat water gobbled precious timber, and piping was in short supply. Most mines had to fabricate their own. By 1901 most of the easy gold along the creeks had been sifted and sluiced away. Capitalists who could afford heavy machinery like hydraulic dredges moved in to the Klondike, buying up blocks of claims. With dredges they were able to make profits from low-grade deposits.

Very few women worked their own claims; Nellie was an exception. It was more usual for women to speculate in claims, trying to buy and sell at the right time. A few women grubstaked prospectors: Mae Melbourne became one of the richest women in Dawson by backing others. Either she was lucky or she had a sure instinct for mining prospects. Nearly seven hundred claims were registered by women in the Klondike, representing about 3 per cent of the total, but most were claims in the name of a wife trying to double her man's prospects, since a miner could record only one claim per creek. A few women owned claims in their own name but did not work them.

Jane Clifford, who arrived about the same time as

Nellie, did reasonably well from her claims, although it is not clear whether she worked them herself. Alfreda Healy, aged nineteen and reckoned to be the prettiest girl in the Klondike, had a valuable claim nine miles (fourteen kilometres) from town. She told E. Hazard Wells, a newspaper reporter, that she would live out there with a relative and superintend the diggings on her claim.[2] She was the daughter of Captain John Healy, a successful Yukon trader, and Alfreda was clearly cut from the same cloth as her parents. Her mother also operated her own claims.

Nellie bought her own first claim on May 3. As an unmarried woman, she was restricted to purchasing claims already in existence. Nevertheless, within six months she held several claims, including a "fraction." A fraction came about because of faulty measuring of a claim and, rather than upset other stampeders by trying to adjust the boundaries, the official surveyors would mark off the fraction and open it for staking. Nellie worked at least some of the claims herself, with some success, as according to reports she filled a tomato can with gold dust. Her prize claim was No. 19 Below, well located near the rich diggings on Bonanza Creek. She bought into it with five partners, but after a year the partners were satisfied with their takings and Nellie bought them out. After her death Fred Lockley told the *Anchorage Daily News* that Nellie had recalled for him, "I took out over one hundred thousand dollars from that claim . . . and I spent every red cent of it buying other claims and prospecting the country. I went out with my dog team or on showshoes all over that district looking for rich claims."[3]

By 1899 about twenty thousand people lived in the Klondike valley, and Dawson had become the largest Canadian city west of Winnipeg, much larger than Victoria or Vancouver. It was pioneer living, but even from one year to the next there were visible changes. In the winter of 1897–98, men and horses had to negotiate around tree stumps in the street and flounder in the mud, and many miners lived in single-room shacks. A year later the streets were straight and many cabins had several rooms. Horses were replacing dogs as pack animals. Dawson could boast two newspapers, the *Klondike Nugget* and the *Yukon Midnight Sun*, five churches, and two banks, the Bank of British North America and the Bank of Commerce. Gold dust was still the usual currency, carried by the miners in their buckskin pokes, but paper money had been shipped in and it was also used.

By the winter of 1898–99 it was possible to eat well. Lynch, coming into town from his mine up in the hills, gave a dinner party, and his guests somehow managed to come in evening dress. The lavish menu offered them a mix of local and imported fare. The grayling and ptarmigan with mushrooms were local, the beef, cheeses, champagne, and wines from Outside. Fresh oysters arrived from Whitehorse by dogsled. Other dinners followed, and Lynch commented that Dawson, no matter how isolated, had become a society town.

Not all the women of Dawson were invited to these dinners. The dance hall girls had been recruited to entertain, and charm gold nuggets out of the pockets of, lonely men who had made good. Prostitution was illegal in Canada but tolerated in Dawson, and the prostitutes, about 150 in number, enjoyed a freedom and respect that was unusual. On the whole, the North-West Mounted Police found them less trouble than the dance hall girls. However, in the spring of 1899 a fire in a brothel, started by a fight between two prostitutes, torched forty other buildings, prompting the police to move the girls out of the business district.

Dawson was never a wild town like the mining camps of the Old West. For one thing, the police mingled with the population, making sure that fights did not get out of hand and that drunks were kept away from the gaming tables. The hardships of daily life and the rigours of travel in the biting cold all contributed to an orderly community. Many of the cheechakos had left families behind and wanted to return home with enough money to pay off debts and keep them in comfort. Some were educated men, and most of them were disinclined to riotous living. Certainly some of the miners escaping from the creeks wanted to have fun, and some spent and gambled lavishly. Gold had come to mean very little to men who struck it lucky.

As in South Africa and some of the mining camps of the American West, it was frequently the entrepreneurs, not the miners, who made money. The cost of living so far from the coast was extremely high, but big profits were possible. A Yukon veteran, Jack Dalton, did extremely well herding in cattle by trail and raft and then selling beef at a dollar twenty-five a pound. The river water at Dawson was not fit to drink, and an entrepreneur made his pile bringing water in by dogsled from a spring in the hills a mile (1.6 kilometres) up the Klondike River. Malamute dogs, native to the north, were in great demand for winter sledding. A good one sold for anywhere between two hundred and fifty and four hundred dollars, but they were expensive to feed, each costing its owner about three dollars a day for chum salmon and other food.

To finance her mining ventures Nellie returned to business. In 1898 she opened a short-order restaurant called the Delmonico, her favourite name for a restaurant. On her own admission, even charging two to six dollars a meal, she "didn't make any fortune. Part of the reason, though, was because if a young fellow was broke and hungry I would give him a meal for nothing."[4] Another restaurant, the Cassiar, followed. Some prospectors who were giving up, disillusioned, sold her their grocery in 1901 at the corner of Second Street and Third Avenue in the basement of the Donovan Hotel. Ownership made Nellie one of Dawson's two women grocery proprietors. The Donovan was not Dawson's premier hotel but it had a good location.

Next to the grocery Nellie opened a room that she called The Prospector's Haven of Retreat. She wanted the miners to have an alternative to the saloons and gambling halls where it was too easy to lose hard-earned money. She was wise enough to offer free coffee and cigars. Her reward was new friendships and, probably, useful tips about claims. Her nephew, Tom, who had arrived during Nellie's first summer in Dawson, was helping her now, both in the restaurant and out at her claims.

As she had done everywhere else she had lived,

Nellie quickly became involved in charitable work. Six weeks after arriving in Dawson she was out fundraising for the small hospital of St. Mary's, which was much too small to serve a growing community. Nellie and a woman friend toured the creeks asking for donations. The *Yukon Midnight Sun* reported, "They were quite successful and speak in grateful terms of the generosity and liberal donations of the miners."[5]

John Clum in his tribute to Nellie noted, "Whatever they gave to Nellie was considered an indirect donation to charity for they were quite sure that sooner or later, their gifts and her winnings would all be disbursed to the needy and afflicted, to churches and hospitals, and, therefore, it was only a matter of time until Nellie would be broke again, and it would be up to them to provide her with another 'stake.'"[6]

St. Mary's was the work of the remarkable Jesuit priest Father William Judge. Frail and ascetic but steely willed, Father Judge arrived in Dawson in May 1897 and, working out of a tent, set about building a church and hospital. He was saddened when the nuns coming by boat from St. Michael were unable to reach Dawson that year because of the low water level in the river. They had to return to Holy Cross, a mission less than 300 miles (483 kilometres) from the coast, to wait for spring breakup.

In that lean winter, when flour sold for a hundred dollars a sack, if it could be found at all, men came down with scurvy and Dawson was short of potatoes. The *Klondike Nugget* commented, "During the winter . . . Father Judge's hospital was crowded with the sick and the frozen. The Father's charity was broad as the earth, and none of the hundreds of applicants were even asked their religious preferences."[7]

Conditions eased slightly for the overworked priest when a Canadian physician, Dr. W.T. Barrett, arrived that summer to take over management of the hospital. Dr. Barrett remained for many years, and he and Nellie became close friends. Later, the Oblate Fathers assumed responsibility for the spiritual care of the parish. In July four Sisters of St. Ann finally reached Dawson, a timely arrival as typhoid broke out early in August. The arrival of three more sisters in late August strengthened the nursing staff. With Father Judge, Nellie had been on the bank of the river to greet the sisters as they stepped ashore. She was glad to have the company of professed servants of God. The sisters had a difficult time during their first year in Dawson. They had no proper accommodation, as patients needed the space they were supposed to have. The hospital physicians and friends visited patients until late, the town dogs howled, and, though weary, the sisters found it hard to sleep in their crowded, makeshift quarters.

Even with help from the sisters and the Oblate Fathers, Father Judge was working too hard for a man of frail physique, and in January 1899 he died of influenza on his forty-ninth birthday. The priest had been greatly loved and respected, even by the agnostics of the community, and he was sincerely mourned. All the stores shut on the day of his funeral, and houses and stores were draped in black.

With the arrival of the nuns Nellie had a meaningful number of Catholic religious with whom she could spend her leisure time. Whenever she could take time away from the mining claims or whatever business she was running at the time, Nellie headed to the hospital to enjoy the company of the sisters. The archives of the order reported, "The sisters of St. Mary's Hospital knew her well. With their knowledge of her true worth, her charity, her purity of life, her faith, her deep Catholicism, they ranked her among living saints. After spending an hour with ready pleasantry and Irish wit, she would say to the sisters, 'Now I must go to the Chapel.' And there she would remain an hour or more."[8]

Outside the religious community Nellie had other friends. Dawson attracted several men she had known in mining camps elsewhere. Ed Schieffelin was in Dawson for a time, and Wyatt Earp visited occasionally to scout opportunities and play faro, although he was based now in Nome. She was pleased by a surprise encounter with her Tombstone friend John Clum, who passed through Dawson in June 1898. He was now a US postal inspector in Alaska and visited Dawson out of curiosity, wanting to compare it to other mining camps he had known. Clum had taken to photography and was working in a darkroom of the town studio when Nellie came in seeking donations for the hospital. It had been fifteen years since their last meeting in Tombstone, "but when the distinct tones of that rich Irish brogue reached my ears I recognized the speaker on the instant, and the nature of her appeal further established her identity." Clum took a rather bad photograph of Nellie outside her store. It shows her looking portly, but Clum, ever her admirer, described her as "robust, active, prosperous and popular."[9]

Popular she was in most quarters, but Nellie ran into legal problems that did not enhance her reputation. Early on, with her nephew Tom and a man named Crowley, Nellie bought a claim on Little Skookum Creek from a Mrs. Jendreau. There was some controversy about the claim, and they agreed to have it surveyed. Unwisely, Nellie decided to ensure a favourable outcome for herself and intimated to Captain H.H. Norwood, inspector of mines, that his friend, the hotelier Belinda Mulrooney, might be given an interest in the claim. From rumours in town, Nellie supposed that they were lovers or at least good friends. The commissioner of the Yukon, William Ogilvie, took charge of the inquiry that followed, and Nellie did not come out of it well. Not only had she indirectly offered a sweetener to a government official, but she had involved Belinda Mulrooney, the premier businesswoman of the Klondike.

No one lightly made an enemy of Belinda. She had arrived in Dawson the year before Nellie, penniless but smart and ambitious. Like Nellie, she traced her roots to Ireland and she was attractive, though for years she kept her distance from men. Belinda realized that men out on the creeks would find it a long trek in the snow to Dawson for food and entertainment so, against advice, she built a hotel out at the Forks, fifteen miles (twenty-four kilometres) from town. The gamble paid off and Belinda made money. She bought claims and proved a tough boss to her workers. Edward Morgan, who laboured on one of Belinda's claims for a while, was fired because he was using a shovel the claim foreman had given him. To Belinda it looked too short, and no excuse was acceptable.

The Jendreau affair was not Nellie's only tangle with the mining authorities. Early in 1899 she filed a claim for a bench placer near Monte Cristo Gulch on Bonanza Creek. The owners of two claims on the same hillside claimed that Nellie had encroached on ground they owned. The two men, William Thompson and M.E. Russell, appealed to the gold commissioner, E.A. Senkler. The commissioner decided that Nellie was in the wrong, even if she had made an honest mistake. In a combative mood, Nellie hired a lawyer to handle an appeal. She had spent at least four thousand dollars on the claim, she had a hired hand working there, and she believed right was on her side. The case dragged on until November 1901. Finally, helped by the intervention of the city surveyor, Nellie was awarded ten claims on another creek by way of compensation. It was not a satisfying result for her. She told Commissioner Senkler that she had not made a cent from her Monte Cristo claim, while Russell had made twenty thousand dollars from the piece he had taken from her.

The following year Nellie was involved in another Bonanza claim case, but this time the law supported her. She sued a man named Jones for seven hundred dollars in the territorial court. Going into partnership on claim No. 21 Below, Nellie had advanced supplies and provisions to Jones and could prove it. When Jones reneged on the contract, she sued for return of funds with interest and got it. Nellie may sound quarrelsome, but lawyers were busy in Dawson; it was a town that thrived on litigation.

Nellie had no fears about heading off into little-known country on her own. She was actively prospecting in 1902 and 1903. Dressed in trousers, mackinaw, and fur-lined cap, she would hitch up a team of dogs, load the sled with provisions, and mush out into the Alsek country. In the southwest corner of the Yukon, the Alsek was a magnificent wilderness of mountains, icefields, and glacier-fed rivers.

Jack Dalton, the tough cattleman and trader, had improved an old Tlingit trail to the interior, and by the late 1890s, pack horses and cattle were being herded along the trail from the Alaskan coast to Fort Selkirk in the Yukon. From Selkirk, rafts and later steamboats connected in a day with the Klondike goldfields.

The Kluane district of the Alsek entered mining history when four men walked into Whitehorse in 1903 with 43 ounces (1.2 kilograms) of gold taken from a stream they named Bullion Creek. Predictably, a small stampede ensued. Most of the optimists came from Dawson, now in its waning years as a gold producer. Tents and then cabins and a large hotel sprang up along Bullion, Sheep, and Ruby creeks. Coarse gold was found in almost every creek in the Kluane mining district, but people who dreamed that the region might eclipse the Klondike were disappointed.

Nellie was in on the search fairly early, buying claims on Bullion, Sheep, and Madeline creeks. Bullion was the most profitable, and Nellie is known to have worked her claim there in the winter of 1904. However, the Kluane district was never a rich producer, and only twenty thousand dollars' worth of gold came out of it that year. When Nellie sold, she may or may not have made a profit. On one occasion, to reach Bullion she walked twenty-one miles (thirty-four kilometres) in a temperature of minus 60°F (-50°C), something few would attempt, and she was then almost sixty years old. On the trail she stayed in roadhouses, which could be very rough. In one, she found herself sharing a room with two others. She was lucky to have the top bunk, because the tier collapsed in the night, sending Nellie crashing down on the occupants of the bunks below. She joked later that the unlucky woman in the bottom bunk was still there.

Even with Dalton's trail, the Alsek was far from Whitehorse and Dawson, and flooding, thawing, and freezing of the creeks made working on the diggings difficult. Geologists concluded that hydraulic machinery was essential for profitable mining; however, one hydraulic operation that was started but never activated on Bullion proved an expensive failure. When a richer deposit was struck forty miles (sixty-four kilometres) to the north, many miners were enticed away. A handful of men hung on, supplementing their income by trapping and guiding.

Although she made these arduous journeys, worse perhaps in summer with its mud and mosquitoes, Nellie had health problems while she lived in Dawson. She was admitted five times in three years to the hospital Father Judge founded, once for an intestinal infection that required major surgery and a three- or four-month hospital stay. Given the hazards of surgery and the anesthesia of the time, she must have had amazing powers of recuperation. On her mother's side Nellie had inherited good genes. When Mrs. Cashman died in California in 1899, she was said to be 100 or 103. This must be an exaggeration, given that 1845 was the year of Nellie's birth, but Mrs. Cashman certainly lived a long life.

As the new century came in, Dawson began to empty. Gold production from the Yukon in 1904 was less than half what it had been only four years earlier. This was the pattern of most mining centres: boom followed by bust. Not only were returns less exciting from the Dawson creeks, but gold had been discovered in Nome on the shores of the Bering Sea, luring prospectors north. To the south the Spanish-American War dominated the news, overshadowing notices that came out of the Klondike.

Nellie liked living in Dawson. For spiritual support she had the company of the town's religious, and she enjoyed a lively social life. She was quoted in her *British Daily Colonist* obituary as saying, "I lived in Dawson City seven years. That was a great place to meet interesting people. I met Joaquin Miller [poet and traveller, who came to the Klondike as a newspaper correspondent], Jack London, Jack Crawford, the poet scout, Robert W. Service, and lots of other well-known people up there."[10] She hung on for a while, but by 1904 she had to acknowledge that Dawson would never be the place it had been. It was now a settled community offering a reasonably comfortable life, but the old excitement had gone, and Nellie preferred excitement and the prospect of riches.

Nolan Creek Valley, 1911, showing miners' cabins in the foreground.
COURTESY OF THE US GEOLOGICAL SURVEY/DR. THOMAS G. NOLAN.

CHAPTER NINE

ALASKA

U NUSUALLY PERHAPS, GIVEN her peripa-
tetic nature, Nellie resisted the stampede to
Nome. She had many friends in Dawson,
she was almost sixty years old, and for a time her
health must have been impaired by the surgery.
Nome did attract her friend Wyatt Earp and many
others, excited by news in 1900 that gold had been
found in the sands at the southern end of the Seward
Peninsula. Prospectors streamed north, some of them
escaping debt collectors in Dawson. An instant town
of around five thousand sprang up in a few months
between the tundra and the Bering Sea. In summer

Nome was a dust bowl; the August rains turned the main streets into mud, and the blizzards of winter were terrible. January temperatures could be minus 50°F (-45°C). The Nome boom lasted several years. Almost fifty million dollars' worth of gold was mined on the Seward Peninsula in that first decade, most of it from the Nome district. Gradually, Nome turned respectable, at least in the sense that prostitution and gambling went underground, and the town acquired a hospital as well as several churches, a seven-teacher school, and a library.

The Nome rush brought Nellie's journalist friend Fred Lockley to Alaska. He had hoped to make his fortune mining, but he was too late and had to settle for work as a postal clerk. At heart Lockley was a writer and, when he was back in Oregon, he became a professional publisher and journalist. His forte was interviewing and writing about the lives of pioneers. A column he wrote for several years for the *Oregon Journal* in Portland was very popular, and one of the celebrities he liked to interview was Nellie. When she came south from Alaska in her later years, Lockley could rely on Nellie for a good story.

Nellie must have realized she was too late to do well from placer mining in Nome, and instead her choice was Fairbanks, the new town in the Tanana

Valley of interior Alaska. Fairbanks grew out of a camp on the banks of the Chena River, a tributary of the Tanana. Its founder was a colourful character, E.T. Barnette, a trader and opportunist who had been stranded in shallow waters 200 miles (322 kilometres) downriver from Tanana Crossing, the hub of the valley and his destination. Two prospectors coming down from the hills in search of food induced him to set up a trading post, later named Fairbanks, despite the fact that it was far from trails and far from the nearest mines in the Alaskan wilderness.

A modest gold strike near Fairbanks in 1902 sparked an exodus from Dawson. Hopeful of a second Klondike, this time in the United States, hundreds of men set off to mush 300 miles (483 kilometres) in the middle of winter. They had no reliable maps and some lacked adequate food and winter gear. When they did reach Fairbanks, very few found wealth; news of the find had been exaggerated. However, the status of Fairbanks was enhanced when Judge James Wickersham mushed in from Eagle, an army post on the Yukon, with a dog team loaded with the records that allowed him to open the Third Judicial District offices. The population of his bailiwick was small, but Wickersham's district was larger than Spain, and he enjoyed the status that went with his command.

In later years, he was elected twice to Congress, representing Alaska well and introducing the first Alaska Statehood Bill in 1916.

Prospectors found meaningful gold in the fall of 1903 on three separate creeks near Fairbanks, although it lay far underground and deep shafts were needed. This time the boom was genuine. By 1905 gold worth six million dollars had been taken out of the Fairbanks district, and by 1907 the town had a population of thirty-five hundred, with maybe four times as many prospecting out in the region. Many of them were old sourdoughs from Dawson.

Hudson Stuck, archdeacon of the Yukon for sixteen years, was dismayed by Fairbanks in its early days. He considered it a place of "feverish trade and feverish vice . . . when the stores were open all day and half the night and the dance-halls and gambling dens all night and half the day."[1] Gold from the creeks came into town once a week escorted by horsemen armed to the teeth. By 1910 the Wild West flavour had largely gone. The placers were being exhausted, but a quartz camp was developing. Well-built houses in town were embellished with gardens, and telephone and railroad connected the creeks with the town.

Arriving in 1904, Nellie came at a propitious moment. She opened a grocery and miners' supply store and it did well. She told Fred Lockley that in a matter of months, she made four thousand dollars. Other newspaper accounts suggest she made six thousand dollars, but four thousand was the sum she mentioned to Lockley. Being Nellie, she thought of what the community needed and, as elsewhere, she set about raising funds for the local hospital. St. Matthew's Hospital came under the auspices of the Episcopal missions, but Nellie's Catholicism was broadminded. She saw only a need that she was uniquely equipped to fill. Nellie became a dear friend to the two Anglican missionaries, Deaconess Clara Carter and Annie Cragg Farthing. Before her arrival they had been trying to run a hospital almost bare of equipment and supplies.

Nellie set off by dog team or boat along the Yukon, touring mining camps for donations. In her memoirs, Clara Heintz Burke, wife of a respected Alaskan medical missionary, noted that Nellie's fundraising activities were unorthodox. She would stop at saloons where men were gambling and wait till the jackpot was a tempting size; then she would sweep the money off the table into her own purse, telling the miners, "Okay, boys! This is for the hospital. You've all had the good of it, you low down blankety-blank varmints—and if you got money to throw away at poker, you can give it to them hard-working Christian women that's taking care of the sick." Apparently Nellie never met with resistance.

Deaconess Carter, a trained nurse, was later posted to the new Episcopal mission of St. John's-in-the-Wilderness at Allakaket, the first mission on the Koyukuk River and home to two villages of Eskimos and Athabascan Indians. Clara Heintz, then a young assistant at the mission, recalled in her memoirs a surprise visit from Nellie in the winter of 1907–08. Clad in men's clothing, Nellie had mushed northwest from Fairbanks with her dog team to stay overnight at the mission before heading back to the goldfields at Nolan Creek. Deaconess Carter was delighted to see her, and Clara never forgot the stocky, middle-aged woman with greying hair whose weather-beaten face was "a battlefield of freckles and wrinkles." Over tea, biscuits, and jam, the women exchanged news, and Clara enjoyed Nellie's stories of her wily stratagems for raising money for the Fairbanks hospital. Impressed by Nellie's kindness and her rough musher's language, Clara commented, "A more colorful and entertaining highwayman never mushed the trails of the Yukon."[2]

Jesuits opened their own hospital, St. Joseph's, in Fairbanks in November 1906. Three nuns from

St. Ann's assisted in the first challenging year. They were not trained nurses but cared for their patients to the best of their ability. The nuns' sleeping quarters were crowded, and the sisters often went hungry, living off the charity of kind-hearted women of the town. The following year they were replaced by nuns of another order with nursing training.

In Fairbanks Nellie ran her grocery store and prospected as time allowed. Her stay lasted less than two years. Fairbanks gave her the chance to run a successful business, but it was not a genuine mining camp. She had been trying to learn all she could about placer gold finds above the Arctic Circle, and when word came south of promising deposits, she decided to sell out and head north to the Upper Koyukuk in the nearly empty hinterland of Alaska. She leased her first claim on a tributary of the Koyukuk River in July 1905 and settled her affairs in Fairbank. At the age of sixty, Nellie was prepared to set off alone to the most northerly mining camps then in existence. This was the start of the last great adventure of her life and it took her into a remote land, but why run a grocery store when there was the tantalizing prospect of riches in a new mining camp?

ALASKA WAS THE least populated state in the United States. At the turn of the century, a census counted only 63,592 people in the whole vast territory; fewer than 5,000 of those were white, and most of them worked for canneries. North of Fairbanks, the land was almost empty of settlements. For people above the Arctic Circle, the lifeline was the Koyukuk River, a south-flowing tributary of the Yukon River. Southwest of the Koyukuk Basin was the Seward Peninsula, known chiefly for the gold mine town of Nome, and to the northwest lay the Brooks Range, a 700-mile (1,100-kilometre) mountain range separating the interior of Alaska from the North Slope. Few white men or even Eskimo hunters had ventured into these magnificent, forbidding mountains, but from time immemorial huge caribou herds had crossed the range in their annual migration.

Travel inland to the Upper Koyukuk from the Pacific coast involved river journeys of about 1,000 miles (1,620 kilometres). Travellers starting from Fairbanks first had to sail west down the Tanana River to the Yukon River, then down the Yukon and on to the Koyukuk. A long and lonely river, the Koyukuk had few rapids and was navigable by steamboat to Bettles, a trading post on the Middle Fork of the river, 85 miles (137 kilometres) south of the Wiseman district where

Nellie settled. North of Bettles low water levels meant that freight had to be transferred to a horse-drawn scow for the last leg of the journey to the goldfields. Archdeacon Stuck, who travelled the north between 1906 and 1920, wrote in his memoirs, "One will travel 350 miles up the Koyukuk before the first white man's cabin is reached."[3]

The Upper Koyukuk goldfields lay on the Middle Fork of the river. Prospectors disillusioned by the working-out of the best claims in the Klondike had been exploring the creeks since the 1890s. Two small camps emerged, at Nolan Creek, a tributary of Wiseman Creek, and Hammond River. A prospector named O.R. Williams found gold in the Nolan Creek area in 1903 and filed the Discovery claim. According to the US Geological Survey, the Nolan Creek field was part of a gold-bearing belt about 80 miles (129 kilometres) in length, running in an east-west direction from the Chandalar Basin through the Koyukuk Basin. At Nolan Creek, the richest gold came from deeply buried frozen gravels, although there were bench deposits along the east side of the valley and placers in shallow gravels, most of which were quickly mined out. As in the Kluane mining district, the greatest problem of the Koyukuk gold belt was its remote location. The costs of freighting in food and mining equipment ate away at profits. Elsewhere, the deposits would have had greater significance.

Nellie probably learned of the Williams find through Votney Richmond, the general manager of the Northern Commercial Company in Fairbanks, which supplied provisions to her grocery. She leased a claim from Richmond in July 1905, the first of many she was to work or trade in the Upper Koyukuk.

En route to her new home, Nellie allowed herself a visit to the Sisters of St. Ann at the St. Peter Claver Mission at Nulato, a small Athabascan settlement on the west bank of the Yukon. A Jesuit mission had been established there in 1887, and twelve years later nuns were sent to open a school. Nellie arrived with a welcome crate of fruit, potatoes, and beef, as well as a gift of money. She spent a few days at the mission, making a spiritual retreat and enjoying evenings with the nuns and priests. She amused the sisters by making the Jesuit priests wade out into the river to retrieve a big log that she thought worth saving. When Nellie gave an order, few argued.

When she reached the Upper Koyukuk, she settled in a log cabin at Nolan Creek. It was six or seven miles (about ten or eleven kilometres) out from the trading post and social centre of Wiseman, situated where Wiseman Creek ran into the Middle Fork of the

Koyukuk River, but Nolan was closer to the claims Nellie acquired. She had neighbours but not many. One of the very few, and perhaps the only other white woman living at Nolan, was Louisa Pingel, a former missionary married to a miner. She and Nellie must have known each other well and presumably enjoyed each other's company. They were both sustained by their faith, they were both good cooks, and they had a sense of humour. Every Sunday Mrs. Pingel either walked or rode her dog team into Wiseman to teach Eskimo children.

Three Swedish prospectors found pay gold at Nolan Creek in the winter of 1907–08, sparking a small stampede. Four years later, production declined, but in 1911 deep gold was located at Hammond River. Some of Nellie's later claims were Cashman Bench, Sullivan Bench, and Fay Gulch. They were well located, close to the richest deposits then known in the region. Nellie was the sole owner of most of her claims, but of others was a joint owner with R.E. (Bob) McIntyre. McIntyre was a local character who liked to entertain social gatherings, singing in his off-key voice. It was a performance that he enjoyed more than his listeners, but they indulged him. McIntyre was entirely trustworthy, and he and Nellie remained friends and partners until her death. A few of Nellie's claims were held jointly with her nephew Mike, still living in Arizona. Some claims Nellie traded, and some she worked herself, but she usually employed two or three men to work for her. She filed a few claims east of Nolan Creek in the Chandalar District in 1906–07, but the best claims had been taken already.

By 1915 the white population of the Upper Koyukuk numbered three hundred. The miners were outnumbered by Eskimos, who had numerous children, and there were a few Athabascan Indians. To live in this distant wilderness land required mental and physical toughness, but Nellie was to spend two decades in the Upper Koyukuk. In this isolated gold belt of the far north, she had found a life that suited her independent spirit, and she said she preferred the climate to the heat of the American southwest.

Robert Marshall, the forester and explorer, spent many months based in Wiseman between 1929 and 1939. He loved the place and described the village enthusiastically as "two hundred miles beyond the edge of the twentieth century."[4] The nearest doctor and hospital were at Tanana, 150 miles (241 kilometres) away or at Fairbanks, 190 miles (306 kilometres) distant. Isolation and cold largely shielded the white population of the Koyukuk from epidemics of flu and diphtheria. Even though winter temperatures varied between minus 50°F and minus 60°F (-45°C and -50°C), by and large the settlers were healthy, and Nellie far exceeded the usual life expectancy of women of her time. Wiseman came to have nearly fifty cabins, a Pioneer Hall for social events, and, thanks to John Clum, a post office. In summer, mail came from Tanana by steamship, boat, and scow. In winter, news from Outside arrived by dog team from Bettles.

The Upper Koyukuk bred a proud people. As Nellie commented, "It takes real folks to live by themselves in the lands of the north."[5] In its isolation, the Upper Koyukuk evolved its own distinctive culture. Marshall concluded it was a place of unusual freedom and even happiness. Prostitutes came and went as camp fortunes ebbed and flowed, but the sourdoughs tended to stay. Commenting on their generosity, Archdeacon Stuck wrote, "There is probably no other gold camp in the world where it is a common thing for the owner of a good claim to tell a neighbour who is 'broke' to take a pan and go down to the drift and help himself."[6]

Even when mining was frustrating in terms of reward, it was to the sourdough meaningful work and never boring. Winter and summer temperatures were so different that a change of seasons brought the interest of a changed lifestyle. The trickiest season for travel was spring when the breakup of ice on the river created mud in town and the trails were soggy. Fatigue was a common complaint in the long daylight of summer, as people took to the hills to pick blueberries or snare rabbits and ptarmigan. Marshall described returning to Wiseman after winter walks when "The southern sky would be brilliant with sunset colors, the snow all around would change from a strange purple to a dark gray, and diminutive Wiseman would be twinkling with lights."[7] Although half the claims were worked in winter, it could be a difficult time, tempting men to abuse alcohol or get into fights. Gatherings at the Wiseman roadhouse made for cheerful interludes in the long dark of winter. The consumption of whisky astonished Archdeacon Stuck, and the Eskimo girls had an amazing stamina for dancing.

For Nellie, the closest nuns and priests were at Nulato. There was no counterpart to the religious community she had known in Fairbanks or Dawson. Five or six other residents of the Upper Koyukuk were nominally Roman Catholics, but it seems none shared her fervour. These were years when Nellie developed her own inner spiritual life, praying with special devotion for souls in purgatory.

While she was reasonably successful mining at Nolan Creek, a great strike, the motherlode, eluded Nellie. She had enough money to move, and though she could have found a caring home with her nephew Mike in Arizona, she stayed on. Like the other miners of Wiseman and the creeks, she had her independence, yet she knew that she could call on others for help in a crisis, just as she was called on. Nellie needed to be needed, and the sourdoughs she called "her boys" loved and respected her.

She was never worried about her safety. She told Lockley that she had never carried a gun and would not know how to shoot one. Lamenting her death in 1925, the *Arizona Daily Star* reported that Nellie had said, "I've been all through Alaska dozens of times but I've never been troubled by bad men. There isn't a man in Alaska who doesn't take off his hat whenever he meets me—and they always stop swearing when I come around too." She acknowledged, "Of course, there are some rascals everywhere, but up north, there is a kindly feeling toward humans and a sense of fair play that one doesn't find here, where men cut each other's business to hack and call it 'competition.'"[8]

Nellie was sure of the respect of others living in the Upper Koyukuk, but life still had its misadventures. Long river journeys to go Outside and return were never free of risk. Returning north in 1907, Nellie travelled in the company of a veteran miner and, as she described it to Lockley later, "I had a funny experience going down the river on a raft. If you know anything about that river [probably the Tanana] you know how many rocks there are in the channel and how swift the rapids are. In any event, coming down through some swift water we struck a submerged rock that wrecked our raft. It knocked all of the middle logs out. All we had left were the two cross pieces and the two outside logs. Sure, we got to shore all right, and fixed up the raft and went on. There is always something interesting happening."[9] Nellie and her companion might have drowned, but she treated the mishap with her customary good humour.

In the summer of 1908 Nellie went south to Fairbanks and was interviewed by the *Fairbanks Daily News-Miner*. She spoke enthusiastically about prospects at Nolan Creek, explaining that she had come south to buy boilers for herself and other miners to inject steam into the permafrost. She had seen boilers eliminate hard labour in the Klondike and knew it was what the diggings of the Koyukuk needed.

Nellie was always a gift to a news reporter. She did not encourage questions about her unmarried state but enjoyed talking and joking about life north of the Arctic Circle. She was always confident she would locate a rich deposit and then, typically, she intended using the profits to give employment to others to pioneer new districts. As for living in a sparsely populated land among men, she told a reporter from the *Fairbanks Daily Times*, "I have prospected in Wyoming and in other states of the West and am now getting to be an old woman, and I can truthfully say that there was never a bigger-hearted or more broad-minded class of men than the genuine sourdoughs of Alaska." [10]

Once the new boilers had been sent north to the Nolan Creek diggings, Nellie took a vacation. From one of the Pacific ports she caught a steamer, sailed south, and then travelled inland to stay with her nephew Mike and his family in Bisbee. The father of six, Mike was doing well. He was now a director of two banks and had served a term as president of the Arizona Bankers' Association. There was a close bond between Nellie and Mike, and on this visit she signed over to him a share in her last claim in Cochise County.

Returning, Nellie stopped off in Fairbanks, where mainly cheering news awaited her. The new boilers were working well although they ate wood insatiably, meaning that miners had to go farther and farther from their claims to cut timber. There was already a shortage of wood for heating and cooking. On one claim coarse gold had been found at 120 feet (37 metres), giving the owners a handsome payoff. Nellie learned that her own No.1 Below claim had hit gold at bedrock, but granite boulders were making it hard to manoeuvre buckets in and out of the shaft. This meant the time and expense of sinking a second shaft. It was frustrating, but Nellie had encountered this kind of setback before.

She was again interviewed by a reporter from the *Fairbanks Daily News-Miner*, and amazed readers learned that she was preparing to cross the Koyukuk Basin in the winter darkness. Nellie's route took her by stagecoach from Fairbanks to Fort Gibbon, an army and trading post at the mouth of the Tanana River. Here she hired a dog team and Indian guide, and mushed north to Coldfoot and finally home to Nolan Creek. It had been a long, gruelling journey from Arizona.

In 1913 the creeks had a good year, with some thirty mines in operation. Gold worth four hundred thousand dollars was recovered, chiefly from Hammond Creek. But the deposits were quickly worked out, and by the following year production was down 35 per cent. Mining in the Upper Koyukuk was becoming expensive. There were no exciting new strikes, and to reach bedrock, shafts had to go deeper and deeper. One of the more profitable years was 1916, and Nellie did quite well from her claims. She felt pleased enough with her mining interests to make another trip to Arizona. This time she went by scow and steamboat to Dawson, where she had a chance to meet with old friends and catch up on their news. Travelling on south, from Whitehorse she was now able to go by train to Skagway, where she boarded a steamship for Seattle.

Early in November Nellie checked in to Seattle's Hotel Northern and was interviewed by the *Alaska Daily Empire*. As one of the very few women working north of the Arctic Circle, she was inevitably news. The reporter described her as a slight little woman with grey hair brushed straight back from her forehead and "big hands roughened and muscular from doing the work of men along the trail and in the camps." Nellie spoke with some amusement of the skirts she had donned for her city sojourn, saying, "These things will go pretty quick when I get back up there. Fine time I'd have with skirts on the trail." [11]

Nolan Creek was so cut off from world events that it was a long time before news of the First World War in Europe reached the camps. When Nellie found out that the United States had entered the war, she spread word along the creeks and persuaded younger men to go and fight. Never one to shirk danger, Nellie declared she would lead a battalion herself. It was November of 1918 and she was seventy-three years old, but she was as good as her word. Off she and her band of patriots set. When they reached Fort Gibbon, hundreds of miles to the south, it was to learn of the armistice, so they returned home, saved from death and trauma in the trenches.

Most winters now Nellie left the Koyukuk for Outside. Sometimes she visited Fairbanks or Juneau, where she had friends. In California she had dental work done, and in Arizona the pull was family. She was finding the winters harder. In December 1920 she spent several weeks with the Sisters of St. Ann, at the hospital they ran in Juneau. She spoke enthusiastically of her mines, and a local newspaper stated that she would be returning to Nolan Creek "to take out another fortune from the paystreak there." [12]

In these years Nellie enjoyed her legendary status as a pioneer woman miner of the north. When she appeared in Seattle or Arizona she gave interviews, advising readers to forget old mistakes, worry less, and take an optimistic view of life. It was all home-spun wisdom but a genuine reflection of her beliefs.

Nellie was justifiably proud of her own grit and stamina. In early January 1921 she told the *Cordova Daily Times*, "I can still drive the dogs and use the snowshoes and no one will ever have the satisfaction of ever having to break trail for me. When I feel that I can no longer keep up I will keep off the trail, but that is many years hence." [13] Stout words from a woman aged seventy-six, but Nellie claimed she had never been overtaken on a long mush.

In the winter of 1921 Nellie headed south to try to raise capital to develop her mines. As an old sourdough she understood that her claims needed machinery for further exploitation. She had taken the precaution of bringing with her several letters of recommendation, believing that these would ease her way into the offices of bankers and investors. The president of the Fairbanks Republican Club, Cecil Clegg, attested to her "great energy and persistence," [14] while Congressman Wickersham wrote a letter on her behalf to the governor of California, asking him to assist her if possible, saying, "She is one of the most capable miners in Alaska, and a woman worthy of the highest credit." [15]

Another tribute she carried with her was from the US marshal for the Fourth Division of Alaska, Lewis T. Erwin. Describing Nellie as "the oldest and most distinguished pioneer woman of the territory," he went on to praise her charitable works. "Besides being a successful miner, Nellie has ever administered to the sick and needy, always wearing the same smile of hope and cheer through sunshine and through shadow, in every camp where she has lived." [16] Despite the accolades, there is no record that Nellie was able to find financial backers. Her reputation was assured, but the Upper Koyukuk was distant and very little known, and the costs of freighting supplies in and ores out were obvious even to those who knew only that the camps were in remote wilderness country.

The lack of financial backing was disappointing, but at this time, friends lobbied for Nellie to be appointed a US deputy marshal for the Koyukuk District. Nellie believed she was qualified for the role, but she demurred, saying, "The law of the two-gun is too severe for me and I wouldn't think of using force on anybody, particularly those boys up there. You see, they look on me as sort of a mother and they wouldn't think of doing anything wrong while I was around." [17] Never appointed, she probably enjoyed hearing that her name had been put forward. It was extremely rare at that time for a woman to be appointed to a senior government position.

Nellie still believed that her claims held significant beds of gold below what she deemed false bedrock, but to reach those deposits she needed hydraulic machinery. To raise capital she formed the Midnight Sun Mining Company in late 1922, offering fifty thousand shares at two dollars each. How many investors bought into her company is not known, though certainly some shares were sold. But still more money was needed. Again, she went south, this time starting with an astonishing river journey from Nolan Creek to Anchorage by dog team.

Nellie mushed the 750 miles (1,207 kilometres) in seventeen days, running behind her dogsled and giving herself breaks by standing on the runners. Presumably she took on new provisions in Fairbanks or Nenana, but she had to carry enough food on her sled to feed the hungry dogs as well as herself. She had to camp in the dark, and battle cold and sleep deprivation. Nellie now wore eyeglasses, and under her warm cap they must have fogged up frequently, a minor but real irritation. Her greatest risk was that if she or one of her dogs were injured on the trail, she would be stranded alone, far from help. On the Yukon and Tanana rivers she had the advantage of the smooth ice that preceded heavy snow. This allowed swift travel, but it was an extraordinary feat for winter and won Nellie, now seventy-seven, the title of champion musher of the North. Praising the exploit, the *Associated Press* noted that Nellie was "of slight figure and worn by years of prospecting and mining in the north." [18]

From a financial point of view, this was another discouraging trip. She had planned to go to New York, but the investor she had hoped to see was away in Florida. Her search for capital may have been doomed from the start: during Nellie's lifetime there was no outside investment in the Upper Koyukuk. It was too much of a risk for capitalists.

A short stay in Arizona left happier memories. Nellie revisited Tucson for the first time in three decades, and gave Bishop Gerche one thousand dollars, hoping it would be spent on improvements to the church in Tombstone, the church whose existence was due to Nellie's initiative and fundraising abilities. As always, the Cunningham family gave her a warm welcome in Bisbee. Over the years Mike had written cheques payable to his aunt. She had deposited them in a bank in Fairbanks, but it seems that few, and perhaps none, were ever cashed. Mike tried hard to persuade her to stay in Bisbee. He was well able to take care of her financially and felt she deserved to rest after years of adventure. Elderly and worn Nellie might be, but she was not ready for a rocking chair on a verandah. She spoke of promising claims that she wanted to develop and the friends who expected her back. Who would encourage "her boys" if she stayed in Arizona, she asked?

By early April Nellie was back home and claimed she felt fine after the long trip. The Northern Commercial Company had arranged a fast dog team and driver to take her inland over the coastal mountains and then along the still-frozen river. By northern standards it was an uneventful journey; the sled turned over only once, rolling her in the snow. Nellie had a second cabin at Wiseman and stayed there, while out at Nolan Creek firewood was cut for her and some repairs were made to her cabin.

Life resumed, Nellie working the claims, and encouraging "her boys," but the following summer she developed serious lung trouble and had to postpone a planned return to the United States. Friends brought her down the Koyukuk in a small boat and then west on the Yukon to the mission at Nulato. It must have been an agonizing journey with every breath causing pain in her lungs. The sisters realized Nellie was very sick, but the mission had no doctor so, in the company of one of the nuns, Nellie was taken on to Fairbanks aboard the *General Jacobs*.

She boarded the boat in Nulato in good spirits and was pleased when the captain arranged a birthday cake in her honour. At Fairbanks Nellie was admitted to St. Joseph's Hospital, run by the Sisters of St. Ann. She had survived a journey of about 1,000 miles (1,600 kilometres), seriously ill with double pneumonia and suffering as well from rheumatism. The medical staff wanted her to have further treatment, and after six weeks Nellie was sent south to Seattle and admitted to Providence Hospital.

At this point Nellie seems to have realized that she would break no more trails in the north country. She asked to be admitted to St. Joseph's Hospital in Victoria and travelled upcoast in the company of Mrs. Adams, the wife of a steamboat captain. Arriving frail and weary, Nellie managed to walk in the front door of the hospital, to be greeted by her old friends the nuns and by Dr. Barrett, whom she knew from her Dawson days. Everyone knew she could not recover. Nellie made arrangements to pay outstanding bills and in early November she dictated a will, appointing Charles Murray and her Nolan Creek friend Bob McIntyre as her executors. Two-thirds of her estate was left to Mike Cunningham and his children, and one-third to Sister Mary Mark of St. Ann's. Her personal effects and some mining properties were bequeathed to the same sister "for charitable purposes."

On the evening of Sunday, January 4, 1925, Nellie died, aged eighty. In the last physically painful weeks she was sustained by her faith and apparently cheered by the prospect of joining old friends Up There. In their company she looked forward to spinning yarns about the adventures of mining. "Why, I bet there's never been yarns like the ones we'll spin when I get there,"[19] Nellie is supposed to have said. Father Anselm Wood, Rector of St. Andrew's Cathedral in Victoria, officiated at the funeral mass on January 7, attended by a few intimate friends and Sisters of St. Ann. The cortège made its way to Ross Bay Cemetery, and Nellie was buried just outside the area reserved for the graves of nuns.

So a valiant life came to an end. Nellie's death from pneumonia was fitting for a northern miner. The disease had killed many men she knew, including the Reverend John Huhn of Rampart. Popularly known as the Flying Parson of the north, Huhn had chaired the committee charged with planning the building of St. Matthew's Hospital in Fairbanks.

News of Nellie's death reached the north and southwest, and tributes poured in. Obituaries appeared not just in the newspapers of mining towns like Dawson, Fairbanks, and Tombstone, but also in leading newspapers such as the *Los Angeles Times*, the *New York Times*, and the *San Francisco Chronicle*. The many tributes tended to emphasize Nellie's compassion for the sick and needy rather than her long career as a miner. Acknowledgment of her role as prospector and grubstaker came from the *Engineering & Mining Journal-Press*. Recalling that Nellie was one of the first women to enter Alaska as a gold prospector, the journal stated that she "was held in high regard by a very wide circle of acquaintances."[20]

On January 6, 1925, the *British Daily Colonist* noted, "Her influence for good was felt wherever she went. She nursed the sick, fed the hungry, and did what she could to make easier the life of her less fortunate fellow beings."[21]

The *Victoria Daily Times* had this to say: "Like many pioneer women who have known the meaning of hardship, she was of a most kindly disposition, nursing the sick and feeding the hungry and doing all she could to help the unfortunate and her death will be sincerely mourned by a wide circle."[22] On January 7 the newspaper ran a follow-up story under the heading "Champion woman musher of the world is buried here." Nellie is described as "one of the first of the daring band of women to enter the frozen, uncharted fields of Alaska."[23] The tribute recalled that Nellie served as nurse at many mining camps, as well as staking her own claims, and noted that she had grubstaked several miners from Tombstone who went on to be millionaires.

In a tribute three days later, the *Times* stated, "She had an amazing personality with a sunny smile and a most infectious laugh, which won her many friends wherever she went." Speaking of Nellie's Dawson days, the report continued, "her entrance into a saloon or dance hall was the signal for every man in the place to stand, such was their high opinion of her. If any man was taken ill, it was her hands that tended him and nursed him through the sickness, and she became a veritable 'Lady of the Lamp' in many a prospector's shanty."[24]

The life Nellie forged for herself on Nolan Creek suited her. She was needed by "her boys" and still certain that a rich vein of gold ran under the creek. Nellie never lost her belief that the far north would yet produce another Klondike. She hoped to make a fortune and use it to finance the further development of mines in the Koyukuk, as well as church causes.

Nellie's mining life spanned sixty years, and in that time the lone prospector of the southwest with his burro gave way to an industry largely dependent on hefty capital investment, mining engineers, and machinery. The Upper Koyukuk was changing too. The old sourdoughs were dying off around the time that Nellie died. A wireless station opened in 1925, allowing communication with Fairbanks, and in May of that year an airplane landed in Wiseman, on the first recorded flight north of the Arctic Circle. The first automobile arrived in 1931, hauling men and mining supplies out to Nolan Creek and Hammond River. Nellie and her mining contemporaries might not have cared for the changes. Returning to the Upper Koyukuk in 1938, Robert Marshall regretted the disappearance of the old-timers and their pioneer traditions.

Nellie has never been forgotten. In 2006 she was inducted into the Alaska Mining Hall of Fame. The following year she was inducted into the National Cowgirl Museum and Hall of Fame in Fort Worth, Texas. In 1994 she was featured on one of the "Legends of the West" stamps of the US Postal Service. Ireland has acknowledged the fame of an emigrant daughter who never forgot the tragedy of the famine: in Midleton, near where she was born, a monument was erected to her memory in 2014. Officially unveiled in June 2015, it extolls "the Angel of the Cassiar Mountains."

ENDNOTES

INTRODUCTION

[1] *British Daily Colonist*, January 11, 1925.

[2] *Fairbanks Daily Times*, July 22, 1908, and *Anchorage Weekly Times*, January 24, 1925.

[3] *British Daily Colonist*, January 11, 1925.

[4] *Klondike Nugget*, April 22, 1900.

[5] *Arizona Daily Star*, January 11, 1924.

[6] *British Daily Colonist*, January 11, 1925.

[7] Woods. *God's Loaded Dice* 64.

[8] Quoted in Clum. *Nellie Cashman* 21.

CHAPTER ONE: EARLY YEARS

[1] Prince Albert to Lord John Russell, April 5, 1848. Quoted in Loughlin, James. "Allegiance and Illusion." *History* 87: 288, October 2002: 491–513.

[2] *Freeman's Journal*, April 12, 1846.

[3] *Cork Examiner*, December 18, 1846.

[4] Clum. *Nellie Cashman* 6.

[5] Brophy, Frank Cullen. "God and Nellie." *Alive*, October 1973: 2–3, 28.

[6] Kemble. *The Panama Route* 160.

CHAPTER TWO: THE SOUTHWEST

[1] *Pioche Daily Record*, October 4, 1872.

[2] Ibid., April 15, 1873.

[3] McKenna. *Black Range Tales* 12.

[4] Brophy. "God and Nellie." *Alive*, October 1973: 3.

[5] *British Daily Colonist*, January 11, 1925, and other sources.

CHAPTER THREE: THE CASSIAR

[1] *Daily British Colonist*, February 5, 1875.

[2] London, Jack. "The White Silence." Short story first published in *Overland Monthly* 33, February 1899.

[3] *Daily British Colonist*, February 5, 1875.

[4] Ibid., March 6, 1875.

[5] Ibid., February 5, 1875.

[6] *Arizona Daily Star*, January 11, 1924.

CHAPTER FOUR: ARIZONA

[1] *Arizona Daily Star*, January 18, 1924.

[2] Bailey, Lynn R., editor. *Tombstone from a Woman's Point of View* 8.

[3] *Daily Arizona Citizen*, July 29 and August 14, 1879.

[4] Clum. *Nellie Cashman* 6.

[5] Ibid., 9.

[6] *Tombstone Nugget*, April 1, 1880.

[7] Ibid., June 24, 1880.

[8] Ibid., October 31, 1880.

[9] *Tombstone Epitaph*, September 25, 1880.

[10] Ibid., November 27, 1881.

[11] Ibid., March 18, 1881.

[12] Clum. *Nellie Cashman* 9.

[13] *Tombstone Nugget*, June 8, 1881.

[14] *Tombstone Epitaph*, October 2, 1881, and *Tombstone Nugget*, November 10, 1881.

[15] *Tombstone Epitaph*, October 4, 1881.

[16] Attributed to Wyatt Earp and frequently quoted in sources such as Myers, John Myers. *Doc Holliday*. Lincoln, NE: University of Nebraska Press, 1973.

[17] *Tombstone Epitaph*, December 17, 1881, and *Tombstone Nugget*, December 31, 1881.

[18] *Tombstone Epitaph*, April 25, 1882.

[19] Ibid., June 1882 advertisements.

CHAPTER FIVE: BAJA AND TOMBSTONE

[1] *San Diego Union*, June 16, 1883.

[2] Ellis, George M. "Sheriff Jerome L. Ward and the Bisbee Massacre of 1883." *Journal of Arizona History* 35, 1994: 315–42, and other sources.

[3] *Tombstone Epitaph*, March 27, 1882.

[4] *Arizona Weekly Citizen*, August 9, 1884.

CHAPTER SIX: RESTLESS FEET

1 *Tombstone Epitaph*, February 3, 1886.

2 Ibid., April 17, 1886.

3 *Arizona Daily Star*, June 29, 1886.

4 McKenna. *Black Range Tales* 149.

5 *London Story Paper*, August 20, 1898.

6 *Arizona Daily Star*, March 6, 1889.

7 *Bisbee Daily Review*, April 1, 1948.

8 *Arizona Daily Star*, November 23, 1889, and *Tombstone Prospector*, November 25, 1889.

9 Ibid., October 24, 1895.

10 *Los Angeles Times*, November 6, 1895.

11 *Arizona Silver Belt*, February 2, 1896.

12 *Arizona Sentinel*, July 24, 1897.

13 Ibid., February 2, 1898.

14 *Tombstone Prospector*, November 19, 1897.

CHAPTER SEVEN: THE KLONDIKE TRAIL

1 *Victoria Daily Colonist*, February 15, 1898.

2 Ibid., March 9, 1898.

3 *Victoria Daily Times*, January 10, 1925.

4 *Victoria Daily Colonist*, January 25, 1898.

5 *British Daily Colonist*, January 11, 1925.

6 Ibid.

7 Woods. *God's Loaded Dice* 64.

[8] Judge, Father William. Letter to his brother from Nulato, June 30, 1894. Quoted in Judge, *An American Missionary*, 124.

CHAPTER EIGHT: DAWSON

[1] Lynch. *Three Years in the Klondike* 84.

[2] Wells. *Magnificence and Misery* 136.

[3] *Anchorage Daily News*, January 19, 1925.

[4] *British Daily Colonist*, January 11, 1925.

[5] *Yukon Midnight Sun*, June 18, 1898.

[6] Clum. *Nellie Cashman* 28.

[7] *Klondike Nugget*, February 1898. Quoted in Judge. *An American Missionary* 211–212.

[8] Theodore, Sister Mary. Unpublished typescript. "The Sisters of St. Ann on North Pacific Shores." Archives of St. Ann. Quoted in Clum. *Nellie Cashman* 111.

[9] Clum. *Nellie Cashman* 24.

[10] *British Daily Colonist*, January 11, 1925.

CHAPTER NINE: ALASKA

[1] Stuck. *Ten Thousand Miles with a Dog Sled* 251.

[2] Burke, Clara Heintz. *Doctor Hap* 91–92.

[3] Stuck. *Ten Thousand Miles with a Dog Sled* 367.

[4] Marshall. *Arctic Village* 9.

[5] *Arizona Daily Star*, January 11, 1925.

[6] Stuck. *Ten Thousand Miles with a Dog Sled* 49.

[7] Marshall. *Arctic Village* 8.

[8] *Arizona Daily Star*, January 11, 1925.

[9] *British Daily Colonist*, January 11, 1925. Story filed by Fred Lockley.

[10] *Fairbanks Daily Times*, July 22, 1908.

[11] *Alaska Daily Empire*, November 2, 1916.

[12] Ibid., December 22, 1920.

[13] *Cordova Daily Times*, January 4, 1921.

[14] Unpublished testimonial letters held by the Sisters of St. Ann, Victoria. Quoted in Clum. *Nellie Cashman* 143.

[15] Ibid.

[16] Ibid.

[17] *Sunset* magazine 46. "Interesting Westerners," May 21, 1921, 48.

[18] Associated Press, January 10, 1924.

[19] Lake. "Irish Nellie." *Alaska Sportsman*, October 1963, 44.

[20] *Engineering & Mining Journal-Press*, January 31, 1925.

[21] *British Daily Colonist*, January 6, 1925.

[22] *Victoria Daily Times*, January 6, 1925.

[23] Ibid., January 7, 1925.

[24] Ibid., January 10, 1925.

ACKNOWLEDGMENTS

[1] Marshall. *Arctic Village* 6.

BIBLIOGRAPHY

Books and Periodical Articles

Backhouse, Frances. *Children of the Klondike.* Vancouver, BC: Whitecap Books, 2010.

Bailey, Lynn R., editor. *Tombstone from a Woman's Point of View: The Correspondence of Clara Spalding Brown, July 7, 1880, to November 14, 1882.* Tucson, AZ: Westernlore Press, 2003.

Basque, Garnet. *Gold Panner's Manual.* 3rd edition. Victoria, BC: Heritage House, 2012.

Bauer, Carolyn. *Ghost Towns of Arizona: Remnants of the Mining Days.* Frederick, CO: Renaissance House, 1988.

Berton, Laura Beatrice. *I Married the Klondike.* Toronto: McClelland & Stewart, 1954.

Berton, Pierre. *Trails of '98.* Toronto: McClelland & Stewart, 1992.

Berton, Pierre. *The Klondike Fever: The Life and Death of the Last Great Gold Rush.* New York: Carroll & Graf, 1958.

Black, Martha Louise. *My Ninety Years.* Edited by Flo Whyard. Anchorage, AK: Northwest Publishing, 1976.

Bolotin, Norm. *Klondike Lost: A Decade of Photographs by Clarke and Clarence Kinsey*. Anchorage, AK: Northwest Publishing, 1980.

Brennan, T. Ann. *The Real Klondike Kate*. Fredericton, NB: Goose Lane Editions, 1990.

Burke, Clara Heintz. *Doctor Hap*. New York: Coward-McCann, 1961.

Cantwell, Sister Margaret. *North to Share: The Sisters of Saint Ann in Alaska and the Yukon Territory*. Victoria, BC: Sisters of St. Ann, 1992.

Chaput, Don. *Nellie Cashman and the North American Mining Frontier*. Tucson, AZ: Westernlore Press, 1995.

Clum, John P. "Nellie Cashman: The Angel of the Camp." Reprinted from *The Arizona Historical Review*, January 1931.

Cole, Terrence. *Crooked Past: The History of a Frontier Mining Camp*. Fairbanks, AK: University of Alaska Press, 1991.

Cole, Terrence. "Nome 'City of the Golden Beaches.'" Jim Walsh, editorial consultant. *Alaska Geographic* 11:1, 1984.

Duncan, Jennifer. *Frontier Spirit: The Brave Women of the Klondike*. Canada: Anchor Canada, 2003.

Enss, Chris. *A Beautiful Mine: Women Prospectors of the Old West.* Guilford, CT: Globe Pequot Press, 2008.

Eppinga, Jane. *Tucson, Arizona.* Charleston, SC: Arcadia Publishing, 2000.

Evans, Polly. *Yukon: The Bradt Travel Guide.* Chalfont St. Peter, England: Bradt, 2010.

Faulkner, Edward L. *Introduction to Prospecting.* Victoria, BC: Geological Survey Branch of the Ministry of Energy, Mines and Petroleum Resources, 1986.

Fischer, Ron W. *Nellie Cashman: Frontier Angel.* Honolulu: Talei Publishers, 2000.

Garvey, John and Karen Hanning. *Irish San Francisco.* Charleston, SC: Arcadia Publishing, 2008.

Gates, Michael. *Gold at Fortymile Creek: Early Days in the Yukon.* Vancouver, BC: University of British Columbia Press, 1994.

Goodwin, John M. "The Panama Ship Canal and Interoceanic Ship Railways Projects." Paper read before the Engineers' Club of Cleveland, Ohio, November 6, 1880 (optical reprint of 1923 publication).

Gordon-Cooper, H. *Yukoners: True Tales of the Yukon.* Vancouver, BC: Riverrun Publishing, 1978.

Gray, Charlotte. *Gold Diggers: Striking It Rich in the Klondike*. Toronto: HarperCollins, 2010.

Greever, William S. *The Bonanza West: The Story of the Western Mining Rushes 1848–1900*. Norman, OK: University of Oklahoma Press, 1963.

Haskell, William B. *Two Years in the Klondike and Alaskan Gold-fields*. Memphis, TN: General Books, 2012 (optical reprint of 1898 original).

Judge, Charles Joseph. *An American Missionary: A Record of the Work of Rev. William H. Judge, S.J.* Maryknoll, NY: Catholic Foreign Mission Society of America, 1907.

Kee, Robert. *Ireland, a History*. London: Weidenfeld & Nicolson, 1980.

Kelly, John. *The Graves Are Walking: The Great Famine and the Saga of the Irish People*. New York: Henry Holt and Company, 2012.

Kelly, Richard J. *Queen Victoria and the Irish Post-Famine Context: A Royal Visit*. Osaka: Kinki University, n.d.

Kemble, John H. *The Panama Route, 1848–1869*. Berkeley, CA: University of California Press, 1943.

Lake, Ivan C. "Irish Nellie: Angel of the Cassiar." *Alaska Sportsman*, October 1963: 44.

Laurence, Frances. *Maverick Women: 19th Century Women Who Kicked Over the Traces.* Carpinteria, CA: Manifest Publications, 1998.

Ledbetter, Suzann. *Nellie Cashman: Prospector and Trailblazer.* El Paso, TX: University of Texas Press, 1993.

Lee, Gwen, and Don Lee. *Rivers of Gold: A True Yukon Story.* Surrey, BC: Hancock House, 2004.

Lynch, Jeremiah. *Three Years in the Klondike.* Edited by Dale L. Morgan. Chicago: R.R. Donnelley & Sons, 1967.

Marshall, Robert. *Alaska Wilderness: Exploring the Central Brooks Range.* 2nd ed. Berkeley, CA: University of California Press, 1973.

Marshall, Robert. *Arctic Village.* New York: Harrison Smith and Robert Haas, 1933.

Martin, T. *Life of the Prince Consort.* London: Smith Elder, 1875–79.

Mayer, Melanie J. *Klondike Women: True Tales of the 1897–1898 Gold Rush.* Athens, OH: Swallow Press/ Ohio University Press, 1989.

McKenna, James A. *Black Range Tales.* Silver City, NM: High-Lonesome Books, 2002 (first published 1936).

McPhee, John. *Coming Into the Country.* New York: Farrar, Straus & Giroux, 1976.

Mole, Rich. *Gold Fever: Incredible Tales of the Klondike Gold Rush*. Victoria, BC: Heritage House, 2009.

Monahan, Sherry. *Taste of Tombstone: A Hearty Helping of History*. Edited by Jennifer Simmons. Ravia, OK: Royal Spectrum, 1998.

Morgan, Murray. *One Man's Gold Rush: A Klondike Album*. Photographs by E.A. Hegg. Seattle, WA: University of Washington Press, 1967.

Morrell, W.P. *The Gold Rushes*. London: Adam & Charles Black, 1940.

Murphy, Claire Rudolf and Jane G. Haigh. *Gold Rush Women*. Anchorage, AK: Northwest Books, 1997.

Myers, John Myers. *Tombstone's Early Years*. Lincoln, NE: University of Nebraska Press, 1950.

O'Cathaoir, Brendan. *Famine Diary*. Dublin: Irish Academic Press, 1999.

Otis, Fessenden N. *History of the Panama Railroad*. New York: Harper, 1867.

Paterson, T.W. *Ghost Towns of the Yukon*. Langley, BC: Stagecoach Publishing, 1977.

Patterson, R.M. *Trail to the Interior*. Victoria, BC: Horsdal & Schubart, 1993.

Porsild, Charlene. *Gamblers and Dreamers: Women, Men and Community in the Klondike*. Vancouver, BC: University of British Columbia Press, 1998.

Quiett, Glenn Chesney. *Pay Dirt: A Panorama of American Gold-Rushes*. New York: D. Appleton-Century, 1936.

Ryan, Dennis P. *A Journey through Boston Irish History*. Charleston, SC: Arcadia Publishing, 1999.

Seagraves, Anne. *High-Spirited Women of the West*. Hayden, ID: Wesanne Publications, 1992.

Stevenson, Marc G. "Looking for Gold: Historic Sites Survey of Kluane National Park, Southwest Yukon." MA thesis. Burnaby, BC: Simon Fraser University, 1979.

Stuck, Hudson. *Ten Thousand Miles with a Dog Sled: A Narrative of Winter Travel in Interior Alaska*. Lincoln, NE: University of Nebraska Press, 1988. Originally published New York: Scribner, 1914.

United States Geological Survey. "Nolan Creek." Mineral Resources On-Line Spatial Data, 2011.

Wells, E. Hazard. *Magnificence and Misery: A First-Hand Account of the 1897 Klondike Gold Rush*. Edited by Randall M. Dodd. Garden City, NY: Doubleday, 1984.

Western Writers of America. *The Women Who Made the West*. New York: Doubleday, 1980.

Wolle, Muriel Sibell. *The Bonanza Trail: Ghost Towns and Mining Camps of the West*. Bloomington, IN: Indiana University Press, 1958.

Woods, Henry F. *God's Loaded Dice: Alaska 1897–1930*. Caldwell, ID: Caxton Printers, 1948.

Wright, Allen A. *Prelude to Bonanza: The Discovery and Exploration of the Yukon*. Sidney, BC: Gray's Publishing, 1976.

Young, Otis E. *Black Powder and Hand Steel: Miners and Machines on the Old Western Frontier*. Norman, OK: University of Oklahoma Press, 1976.

Zanjani, Sally. *A Mine of Her Own: Women Prospectors in the American West, 1850–1950*. Lincoln, NE: University of Nebraska Press, 1997.

Zuehlke, Mark. *The Yukon Fact Book*. Vancouver, BC: Whitecap Books, 1998.

Newspapers

Alaska Daily Empire

Anchorage Daily News

Anchorage Weekly Times

Arizona Daily Star

Arizona Gazette

Arizona Sentinel

Arizona Silver Belt

Arizona Weekly Citizen

Bisbee Daily Review

British Daily Colonist

Cordova Daily Times

Cork Examiner (Ireland)

Daily Arizona Citizen

Daily British Colonist

Fairbanks Daily News-Miner

Fairbanks Daily Times

Freeman's Journal (Ireland)

Klondike Nugget

Oregon Journal

Phoenix Daily Herald

Pioche Daily Record

San Diego Union
Tombstone Epitaph
Tombstone Nugget
Tombstone Prospector
Tucson Daily Citizen
Victoria Daily Colonist (title varied over time)
Victoria Daily Times
Yukon Midnight Sun

Periodicals

Alaska Sportsman
Alive magazine
Engineering & Mining Journal-Press
London Story Paper
Sunset magazine

ACKNOWLEDGMENTS

IT HAS BEEN a privilege to research the life of this remarkable woman, Nellie Cashman, and attempt to see that life in the context of the times in which she lived. I am greatly indebted to Don Chaput, whose 1995 biography *Nellie Cashman and the North American Mining Frontier* is both a painstaking and very readable work. For an understanding of life on the Upper Koyukuk in Alaska, I acknowledge my debt to the research of Robert Marshall, forester and conservationist, who explored the Arctic wilderness from 1929 until his untimely death ten years later. His 1933 book *Arctic Village* is an engaging record of the months he spent living among "the people of the Koyukuk who have made for themselves the happiest civilization of which I have knowledge."[1] I am also indebted to James A. McKenna, pioneer of the American Southwest, whose stories, first published in 1936 as *Black Range Tales*, gave me a sense of life in the heady early days of Kingston, a silver-mining town in New Mexico that was Nellie Cashman's home for a while. Garnet Basque's *Gold Panner's Manual*, first published in 1974, is an excellent introduction to prospecting and panning for gold.

We live in the digital age and appreciate its benefits for research. Photographs reproduced in this book courtesy of BC Archives in Victoria were selected from its Photographs and Documentary Art collection. Newspaper Archives Online allowed me to access old newspaper stories, and many times I turned to the Internet for help in checking facts.

Warm thanks go to my publisher, Taryn Boyd, and her team at TouchWood Editions for making this book possible. I was fortunate to have Marlyn Horsdal as my editor. Her recommendations greatly improved the structure and readability of the book. My in-house editor at TouchWood, Renée Layberry, book designer Pete Kohut, promotions coordinator Tori Elliott, indexer Janice Logan, and proofreader Sarah Weber all steered us through the last stages of publishing and the early stages of promotion with skill and enthusiasm. Authors and publishers believe in selling books, and we appreciate the good services of the TouchWood sales team.

Writing is a lonely craft, but I was always cheered by the kindly interest of family and friends. My husband, Roy, was a loyal supporter and helpful critic. Among friends I am especially grateful to Danda Humphreys, Victoria-based author and historical storyteller-guide, for her encouragement and sensible advice.

Archivists, historians, and others patiently answered my queries. My thanks go to Laura Hoff, archivist of the Arizona Historical Society; historian Cindy Hayostek of the Douglas (Arizona) Historical Society; Cherie Salmon of High-Lonesome Books (New Mexico); Sandra M. Johnston of the Alaska State Library; Gloria Kirton of the US Geological Survey; Carey Pallister, archivist of the Sisters of St. Ann, Victoria, British Columbia; Rita Fichtner, office manager of St. Andrew's Cathedral, Victoria, British Columbia; and Sharon Walker, manager of the Sidney, British Columbia, branch of the Vancouver Island Regional Library system. I am grateful to them all.

Paul Larkin of Paul's Computer Services of Sidney, British Columbia, rescued me from several computer crises, usually at short notice. His expertise is appreciated.

INDEX

PHOTO BY MICHELLE ALGER / STUDIO 282 PHOTOGRAPHIC

THORA KERR ILLING is a former journalist and librarian. She immigrated to Canada as a young woman and fell in love with the space, the fjords, and the forests of the west. Now retired, she lives in Sidney, BC, and loves travel, books, nature, and animals.